RAT IN THE SKULL

Ron Hutchinson

The Royal Court Writers Series published by
Methuen Drama in association with
the Royal Court Theatre

Royal Court Writers Series

Rat in the Skull was first published in Great Britain
in the Royal Court Writers Series in 1984
by Methuen London Ltd
in association with the Royal Court Theatre
Sloane Square, London SW1N 8AS.
This revised edition published in 1995
by Methuen Drama
an imprint of Reed International Books Ltd
Michelin House, 81 Fulham Road, London SW3 6RB
and Auckland, Melbourne, Singapore and Toronto
in association with the Royal Court Theatre and
the Duke of York's Theatre, London
and distributed in the United States of America
by Heinemann, a division of Reed Elsevier Inc.
361 Hanover Street, Portsmouth, New Hampshire NH 03801 3959

ISBN 0–413–70350–9

A CIP catalogue record for this book
is available from the British Library

Cover design by Paradigm & The Loft
Cover photograph by Eric Richmond

Typeset by Wilmaset Ltd, Birkenhead, Wirral
Printed and bound in Great Britain by
Cox & Wyman Ltd, Reading, Berkshire

Royal Court Theatre Productions Ltd
Duke of York's Theatre Ltd   The Theatre of Comedy Company
Dodger Productions
present
The Royal Court Classics Season

John Castle

Tony Doyle

Pearce Quigley

Rufus Sewell

RAT IN THE SKULL

by **Ron Hutchinson**

Director **Stephen Daldry**

Designer **William Dudley**

Lighting Design **Rick Fisher**

Music **Stephen Warbeck**

Sound Design **Paul Arditti**

Rat in the Skull was first staged at the Royal Court Theatre on 31 August, 1984.
First performance of this production at the Duke of York's Theatre, as part of the
Royal Court Classics Season, 5 October, 1995

The Duke of York's Theatre St Martin's Lane London WC2N 4BG
Sole Proprietor and Licensee The Duke of York's Theatre Ltd
Directors Sir Eddie Kulukundis OBE (Chairman) Howard Panter (Managing Director)
Peter Beckwith David Beresford Jones Robin Guilleret Rosemary Squire Miles Wilkin

Royal Court Theatre Productions Ltd Sloane Square London SW1 8AS
Chairman John Mortimer CBE QC Artistic Director Stephen Daldry
General Manager Vikki Heywood Directors Stuart Burge CBE Anthony Burton
Graham Cowley Harriet Cruickshank Robert Fox Sonia Melchett Alan Rickman
Max Stafford-Clark James L Tanner

Season sponsored by

Royal Court Classics Season

Three plays from the extraordinary list of world renowned playwrights to have been premiered over the past decades by the Royal Court are now presented at the Duke of York's Theatre in this first Season of Royal Court Classics.

This Season of landmark plays gives the Royal Court its third stage and a significant presence in the West End, and gives audiences the chance to experience three of the Royal Court's most celebrated successes.

The Classics Season begins with this production of Ron Hutchinson's *Rat in the Skull*, directed by Stephen Daldry, Artistic Director of the Royal Court, continues with the return of Phyllida Lloyd's production of Terry Johnson's hilarious hit *Hysteria* (winner of the 1994 Olivier Award for Best Comedy), before David Storey's epic *The Changing Room* directed by James Macdonald brings the Season to a close.

23 November 1995 - 27 January 1996

Hysteria

by **Terry Johnson**
Director **Phyllida Lloyd**
Designer **Mark Thompson**
Lighting Design **Rick Fisher**
Sound Design **Paul Arditti**

1 February - 30 March 1996

The Changing Room

by **David Storey**
Director **James Macdonald**
Sound Design **Paul Arditti**

Duke of York's Box Office 0171 836 5122
Royal Court Box Office 0171 730 1745

RAT IN THE SKULL

by **Ron Hutchinson** (1984)

Cast in alphabetical order

Detective Superintendent Harris, Metropolitan Police
John Castle

Detective Inspector Nelson, Royal Ulster Constabulary
Tony Doyle

Constable Naylor, Metropolitan Police
Pearce Quigley

Roche, detainee under the Prevention of Terrorism Act
Rufus Sewell

Director **Stephen Daldry**

Designer **William Dudley**

Lighting Design **Rick Fisher**

Music **Stephen Warbeck**

Sound Design **Paul Arditti**

Production Manager **Iain Gillie**

Company Stage Manager **Sheena Linden**

Deputy Stage Manager **Emma Basilico**

Costume Supervisor **Jennifer Cook**

Wardrobe Supervisor **Cathryn Johns**

Production Electrician **Jerry Hodgson**

Voice Coach **Joan Washington**

Assistant Director **Raeda Ghazaleh**

❧ Evening Standard

What building has been more important to the culture of modern London - or indeed to modern drama anywhere? Since George Bernard Shaw challenged Edwardian Britain from the Royal Court, the theatre has been the brilliant bad boy of British drama, shocking and entertaining generations of Londoners.

It's the theatre we've always gone to for new ideas and new faces, to be in the know and to be outraged. For almost 40 years, since George Devine took Sloane Square in hand, if you didn't have a view on what was going on at the Court, you could hardly claim to be a theatregoing Londoner.

It's a unique London theatre not least because of its location, a wonderfully tatty building atop the tube line between stuffy Belgravia and the artificial Bohemia of the King's Road - an anachronistic yet peculiarly appropriate site. Not a Shaftesbury Avenue theatre but a crucial influence on the slower-thinking West End, as the dozens of successful transfers, from Arnold Wesker's *Roots* in 1959 to David Mamet's *Oleanna* in 1993 (both to the Duke of York's), have shown.

So why move into the West End? At the Evening Standard we think it is a brave and yet pragmatic move - and we have a long history of supporting such initiatives in the arts. It's the right move because the West End, stultified at the moment by commercial pressure and in fear of 'Broadwayisation', needs the Court - to remind it that theatre must challenge and thrill to survive. And the Court needs the West End - in these days no arts organisation can sit on its artistic integrity and allow others to exploit its successes. The Royal Court, with what I hope is just the first of many Classics Seasons, must remind us why we need theatre - and in doing so finance more work to rival what you will see here at the Duke of York's.

Stewart Steven Editor of the Evening Standard

A walk up the alley

ROYAL
COURT
THEATRE
at the
DUKE OF
YORK'S
THEATRE

When I first worked at the Royal Court the bar next door hadn't yet been Bistrofied - it remained a hard drinking holdover where faded photographs of B. Shaw and others looked down on a bear pit of actor desperadoes, their hangers-on and the most Unsloanely of SW Ones. Boisterous would be the word.

Into this stew I proceeded one night with the all-Irish cast of a play previous to RAT. Drink was taken, controversy with the regulars ensued on Irish affairs, currently in a more than usually bloodily explosive phase. Our leading actor polemicist, fresh from Dublin, fell into dispute with a parcel of wiry young men with very very very short hair. These were not, unfortunately for him, Chelsea fans on parole but squaddies from the barracks adjacent, fresh from Belfast. There was no meeting of minds.

The bar was cleared and discussion continued in doorway, on pavement and down that narrow dark alleyway crammed with bins that leads to the Court's stage door, where our most impassioned debater was felled by a blow that gave him a hairline fracture of the skull.

Life had met art; theory of government had met its practitioners and where more apt than at the Court - Mecca for troublemakers, for the impassioned, for those who can't conceive of art that isn't in some way political, worth getting into an argument over.

This play is an argument between nationalist Roche and loyalist Nelson, the committed but wearying Englishman Harris and the uncommitted Englishman Naylor - it's also yrs. truly arguing with himself, trying to square his Northern Irish Protestant heritage with a deeper sense of all-Irishness, setting his head against his heart, trying to find a position.

Step into the alley. The boys are waiting ...

Ron Hutchinson August 1995

The Company

Ron Hutchinson (Writer)
Theatre includes: Says I, Says He (Sheffield Crucible Studio, Royal Court Theatre Upstairs, 1978; Phoenix Theatre, New York, 1979; Mark Taper Forum, Los Angeles; George Devine Award, 1978); The Irish Play (RSC, 1980/81); The Dillen (RSC, 1983/84); Rat in the Skull (Royal Court, 1984 & 1985; Public Theatre, New York; John Whiting Award, 1984; Olivier Award and Critics' Circles Awards in New York, Los Angeles and Chicago); Babbitt! A Marriage (Mark Taper Forum, Los Angeles, 1987); Pygmies in the Ruins (Lyric Theatre, Belfast; Royal Court, 1992).

Television includes: The Out of Town Boys, The Last Window Cleaner and Deasey (Desperate) (BBC, 1979); The Winkler (Thames, 1979); Bull Week (BBC, 1980); Bird of Prey (BBC, 1982 & 1984); Connie (Central, 1985); Rat in the Skull (Central, 1987); The Marksman (BBC, 1987); Murderers Among Us (TVS & HBO, 1988; Emmy Award for Best Teleplay, the International Film and TV Festival Award, the Prague International TV Festival Award and the Simon Weisenthal Foundation Award for Good Works in the Media); Dead Man Out (HBO, 1989; ACE Award for Best Teleplay); The Josephine Baker Story (Anglia & HBO, 1991; five Emmy Awards including Best Director); Against the Wall (HBO, 1993; Emmy Award for Best Director); Fatherland (HBO, 1994); The Burning Season: The Life and Death of Chico Mendes (Enigma Films & HBO, 1994; the Humanitas Prize for Writing, three Golden Globe Awards); The Tuskegee Airmen (Frank Price & HBO, 1995).

Radio includes: Roaring Boys; Murphy Unchained; There Must Be a Door; Motorcade; Risky City; Troupers; Larkin; Pygmies in the Ruins.

Paul Arditti (Sound Designer)
For the Royal Court: Not a Game for Boys; Mojo; Simpatico; The Steward of Christendom; The Strip; Uganda; The Knocky; Blasted; Peaches; The Editing Process; Babies; Some Voices; Thyestes; My Night with Reg; The Kitchen; The Madness of Esme and Shaz; Hammett's Apprentice; Hysteria; Live Like Pigs; Search and Destroy.

Other theatre sound design includes: The Threepenny Opera (Donmar Warehouse); Hamlet (Gielgud); Piaf (Piccadilly); St Joan (Strand & Sydney Opera House); The Winter's Tale, Cymbeline, The Tempest, Antony & Cleopatra, The Trackers of Oxyrhynchus (Royal National Theatre); The Gift of the Gorgon (RSC and Wyndham's); Orpheus Descending (Theatre Royal, Haymarket, and Broadway); A Streetcar Named Desire (Manchester Royal Exchange); The Wild Duck (Phoenix); Henry IV, The Ride Down Mt Morgan (Wyndham's); Born Again (Chichester); Three Sisters, Matador (Queen's); Twelfth Night, The Rose Tattoo (Playhouse); Two Gentlemen of Verona, Becket, Cyrano de Bergerac (Theatre Royal, Haymarket); Travesties (Savoy); Four Baboons Adoring the Sun (Lincoln Center, 1992 Drama Desk Award).

Opera includes: Gawain (Royal Opera House).

TV includes: The Camomile Lawn.

John Castle
For the Royal Court: Saved; The Voysey Inheritance.

Other theatre includes: a season with Prospect Theatre Company; The Merchant of Venice (London Shakespeare Company tour of East Africa); Infidelities (Boulevard Theatre); Breaking the Code (Comedy Theatre); The Wars of the Roses (English Shakespeare Company); Hamlet (Royal National Theatre); When the Past is Yet to Come (Finborough); Zanna (Greenwich Studio).

Films include: Michelangelo Antonioni's Blow-Up; The Lion in Winter; Antony and Cleopatra; Made; Man of La Mancha; Eliza Fraser; Eagle's Wing; King David; Franco Zeffirelli's The Sparrow.

Television includes: The Fight Against Slavery; Ben Hall; I Claudius; The Prime of Miss Jean Brodie; The Professionals; Lillie; Travels with a Donkey; The Wings of a Dove; The Three Hostages; Tales of the Unexpected; Reilly; Sherlock Holmes; Miss Marple; Lost Empires; Tecs; Inspector Morse; Little Lord Fauntleroy; Lovejoy.

Stephen Daldry (Director)
Artistic Director of the Royal Court Theatre since 1993.

For the Royal Court: The Editing Process; The Kitchen; Search and Destroy.

For the Royal National Theatre: Machinal (four 1994 Olivier Awards including Best Director); An Inspector Calls (transferred to the Aldwych; 1992 Evening Standard Award; four 1993 Olivier Awards including Best

Director; 1994 Broadway production won four Tony and seven Drama Desk Awards; has also toured to Australia, Austria and Japan.

For the Gate Theatre: Artistic Director, 1989-92; Spanish Golden Age (1992 Olivier Award for Outstanding Achievement); Prudential Award 1991; Consummate Classics (1990 Time Out Award); Damned for Despair (Best Production and Best Director London Fringe Awards, Time Out Award, Critics Circle Award for Best Director); The Ingolstadt Plays (with Annie Castledine; Time Out, Peter Brook Award); Figaro Gets Divorced; Jerker.

Other theatre includes: Rousseau's Tale (RSC Fringe); Judgement Day (Old Red Lion; 1989 London Fringe Best Production); Badlands (BAC); The Ragged Trousered Philanthropist (Stratford East and Liverpool Playhouse); It's A Bit Lively Outside, The True Story of the Titanic, Cider with Rosie (Crucible Theatre, Sheffield, as Associate Artist). Regional productions at Manchester, Library and Wythenshawe, York Theatre Royal, Liverpool Playhouse, Oxford Stage Company, Brighton Gardner.

Opera includes: Manon Lescaut (Dublin Opera Festival).

Tony Doyle
Theatre includes: Cavalcaders (Abbey Theatre and Royal Court); The Gigli Concert (Abbey Theatre and Almeida); Too Late for Logic (Abbey Theatre); Old Year's Eve (RSC); City Mission (Dublin Theatre Festival); Translations (Hampstead and RNT); The Shadow of a Gunman (Crucible Theatre, Sheffield); John Bull's Other Island, Da (Greenwich Theatre); The Plough and the Stars (RNT); The Birthday Party; Mr Joyce is Leaving Paris.

Television includes: Ballykissangel (World Productions/BBC); Castles, Parole, Headhunters, Between the Lines, Underbelly, Arise and Go Now, A Murder in Eden, Children of the North, The Hen House, Here is the News, Shadow of the Noose, The Contractor, The Nightwatch, Crossfire, Vanity Fair, The Venus de Milo Instead, Book Mark - Samuel Beckett, Danny, Slip Up, Frankie and Johnnie, McCabes Wall, My Brother Jonathan, The Long March, A Woman Calling, One by One, Stay, The Waiting War, Medical Ethics, Two Weeks in Winter, Macbeth, Moving on the Edge, Soft Targets, After the Party, Beloved Enemy, Red Roses for Me, The Enigma Files, 1990, King of the Castle, According to Hoyle (BBC); Band of Gold, Maigret, Hostages, Who Bombed

Birmingham (Granada); Firm Friends (Zenith); The Treaty (TV Film RTE); Lovers of the Lake (RTE); Great Writers - James Joyce, South Bank Show - George Higgins (LWT).

Films include: Circle of Friends; Damage; Secret Friends; Devil's Paradise; Eat the Peach; Walter; Who Dares Wins; Loophole.

William Dudley (Designer)
For the Royal Court: Small Change; Hamlet; Edmond; Kafka's Dick; Etta Jenks.

For the Royal National Theatre: Lavender Blue; Larkrise to Candleford; Lost Worlds; The World Turned Upsidedown; Spirit of '76; Undiscovered Country; Dispatches; Don Quixote; Schweyk in the Second World War; The Mysteries; The Real Inspector Hound; The Critic; Entertaining Strangers; Waiting for Godot; The Shaughraun; Cat on a Hot Tin Roof; The Voysey Inheritance; The Changeling; Bartholomew Fair; The Crucible; The Coup; Pygmalion; The Rise and Fall of Little Voice; Under Milk Wood; Wild Oats.

For the Royal Shakespeare Company: Ivanov; That Good Between Us; Richard III; The Party; Today; The Merry Wives of Windsor; Richard II; A Midsummer Night's Dream.

For the Neue Schauspielhaus, Hamburg: Hamlet.

For Govan Ship Yard, Glasgow: (Cultural Capital of Europe Festival 1990): The Ship; The Big Picnic by Bill Bryden (1994) - both recorded for television.

For London's West End: I Claudius; Mutiny!; Kiss Me Kate; Girlfriends; Matador; Heartbreak House; My Night With Reg.

Opera includes: Anna Christie; The Barber of Seville; Idomeneo (Welsh National Opera); Billy Budd (Metropolitan Opera); Seraglio (Glyndebourne); Tales of Hoffman, Der Rosenkavalier, Don Giovanni, The Cunning Little Vixen (Royal Opera House); The Ring Cycle (Bayreuth); Un Ballo in Maschera (Salzburg Festival); Lucia di Lammermoor (Lyric Opera of Chicago and Paris Opera).

Film: Roger Michell's Persuasion.

Rick Fisher (Lighting Designer)
For the Royal Court: The Queen & I; Hysteria; King Lear; Six Degrees of Separation (also West End); Three Birds Alighting on a Field; Bloody Poetry; Serious Money (also West End and Broadway); A Mouthful of Birds.

Other recent theatre includes: Macbeth (Greenwich); An Inspector Calls (RNT, Aldwych, Broadway, Tokyo and Australia); Under Milk Wood, What the Butler Saw, Pericles, Machinal (RNT); Something About

Us (Lyric Studio, Hammersmith); The Threepenny Opera, The Life of Stuff (Donmar Warehouse); The Cryptogram (Ambassadors); Much Ado About Nothing (Queen's); The Blue Macushla (Druid Galway); The Gift of the Gorgon (RSC and Wyndham's).

Opera includes: Cosi Fan Tutte (WNO);The Magic Flute (Parma); Gloriana, La Boheme, L'Etoile, Peter Grimes (Opera North); Manon Lescaut (Dublin); and three seasons of outdoor operas in Batignano, Italy. Upcoming projects include: The Fairy Queen (ENO); Swan Lake (AMP at Sadler's Wells); Hysteria (Royal Court Classics Season at the Duke of York's). Received nominations for Olivier Awards in 1995 and 1993. In 1994 won the Olivier Award for his work on Machinal, Moonlight and Hysteria; and the Tony and Drama Desk Awards for the Broadway production of An Inspector Calls. Is currently Chairman of the Association of Lighting Designers.

Pearce Quigley
For the Royal Court: Road; The Queen and I (transferred to the Vaudeville); Downfall; Etta Jenks.

For the Royal Shakespeare Company: A Jovial Crew; A Winter's Tale; The Merry Wives of Windsor; The Changeling. Other theatre includes: Rope (Birmingham Rep); Der Neue Menoza (Gate Theatre); Cider with Rosie, Lady From the Sea, Twelfth Night, Red Riding Hood, The Good Woman of Setzuan, Solonila, Animal Farm (Duke's, Lancaster); Richard II (Ludlow Festival); A Winter's Tale, The Park (Crucible, Sheffield); School for Clowns (Sadler's Wells); Abingdon Square (Shared Experience - Soho Poly/Cottesloe Theatre); Hot Fudge and Ice Cream (Contact, Manchester); Lives of the Great Poisoners (Second Stride); The Pied Piper (Birmingham Rep).

Television and film includes: Inspector Morse; Killing Dad; Ladder of Swords; A Perfect Hero; Growing Rich; Prime Suspect 3; How to Speak Japanese; Pie in the Sky.

Rufus Sewell
Theatre includes: Royal Hunt of the Sun; Comedians (Compass Theatre Company); The Lost Domain (Watermill Theatre, Newbury); Peter and the Captain (Battersea Arts Centre); Pride and Prejudice (Royal Exchange Theatre, Manchester); The Government Inspector; The Seagull; As You Like It (Crucible Theatre, Sheffield); Making It Better (Hampstead and Criterion Theatres); Arcadia (Royal National Theatre);Translations (The Plymouth Theatre, New York).

Television includes: The Last Romantics (BBC); Gone to Seed (Central); Cold Comfort Farm (BBC); Middlemarch (BBC); Dirty Something (Skreba); Citizen Locke.

Film includes: Twenty One; Dirty Weekend; A Man of No Importance; Carrington; Victory.

Stephen Warbeck (Music)
For the Royal Court: Mojo; Simpatico; The Editing Process; Some Voices; The Kitchen; Blood; A Lie of the Mind; Greenland; Bloody Poetry; Built on Sand; Royal Borough; Downfall.

Other theatre music includes: An Inspector Calls (transferred to Broadway, Australia, Austria and Tokyo); Machinal; At Our Table; Roots; Magic Olympical Games (Royal National Theatre); The Taming of the Shrew; The Cherry Orchard (RSC); Damned for Despair; Figaro Gets Divorced; The Ingolstadt Plays (Gate Theatre); Canterbury Tales (Crucible Theatre, Sheffield); Judgement Day (Old Red Lion).

Recent television music includes: Prime Suspect (BAFTA Nomination); The Changeling; Skallagrig (BAFTA Nomination); Femme Fatale; You Me & Marley; Bitter Harvest; In the Border Country; Roots; Nona; Happy Feet; Bambino Mio; Meat; Blood & Water; Devil's Advocate; Bramwell; The Chemistry Lesson.

Film scores include: The Mother; Sister My Sister; O Mary This London; Marooned; Crossing the Border; Brothers In Trouble.

Has also written music for many BBC Radio plays and writes for his band, The hKippers.

Royal Court Theatre Productions Ltd (Co-Producer)
Was formed to expand the work of the English Stage Company in the West End, with any profits covenanted to support the work at Sloane Square.

Its first transfer was Caryl Churchill's Serious Money to the Wyndham's in 1987, followed by Timberlake Wertenbaker's Our Country's Good to the Garrick in 1989, Ariel Dorfman's Death and the Maiden to the Duke of York's in 1992, Six Degrees of Separation by John Guare to the Comedy, also in 1992, and David Mamet's Oleanna again to the Duke of York's, and Kevin Elyot's My Night With Reg to the Criterion, both in 1994.

Dodger Productions (Co-Producer)
Is a theatrical partnership comprising Michael David, Doug Johnson, Rocco Landesman, Des McAnuff, Edward Strong

and Sherman Warner, who work together in various combinations. Originating at New York's Brooklyn Academy of Music in 1978, the Dodgers produced Gimme Shelter, Holeville, Emigres and The Bread and Puppet Theatre before migrating to the New York Shakespeare Festival, where they produced Mary Stuart and How it All Began.

On Broadway, some of the award-winning productions for which they have been responsible are: Hamlet starring Ralph Fiennes with the Almeida, The Who's Tommy, Alan Menken's A Christmas Carol, Guys and Dolls directed by Jerry Zaks, The Secret Garden, Jelly's Last Jam, Craig Lucas' Prelude to a Kiss, Roger Miller's Big River, Stephen Sondheim's Into the Woods, Pumpboys and Dinettes and The Gospel at Colonus. Current productions on Broadway are How to Succeed in Business Without Really Trying starring Matthew Broderick, directed by Des McAnuff, and Disney's Beauty and the Beast which opened in April, 1994 (for which they provide general management).

David Strong Warner, Inc is the management company that administers Dodger Productions. D Tours is an affiliate company which books and markets touring attractions. Another related company of the Dodgers restored and now operates the Goldenrod Showboat, a national landmark, in St Charles, Missouri.

The Duke of York's Theatre Ltd
(Co-Producer) in conjunction with the Turnstyle Group Ltd
Award-winning plays presented at the Duke of York's Theatre under the current management include the Royal Court Theatre's productions of Ariel Dorfman's Death and the Maiden and David Mamet's Oleanna, directed by Harold Pinter; Jonathan Harvey's Beautiful Thing; and the Royal National Theatre's production of Arthur Miller's Broken Glass.

The Turnstyle Group's recent productions include the multi award-winning West End premiere of Oscar Hammerstein II's Carmen Jones, directed by Simon Callow at The Old Vic and on UK and Japanese tours; Jonathan Harvey's award-winning comedy Beautiful Thing; A Slip of the Tongue starring John Malkovich; Shades starring Pauline Collins; Single Spies, the award-winning double bill by Alan Bennett, starring Simon Callow, Prunella Scales and Alan Bennett himself; Frankie and Johnny in the Clair de Lune starring Julie Walters and Brian Cox; Look Back in Anger with Kenneth Branagh and

Emma Thompson; the Renaissance Theatre Company's Shakespeare season starring Kenneth Branagh and directed by Dame Judi Dench, Geraldine McEwan and Sir Derek Jacobi; The Common Pursuit by Simon Gray starring Stephen Fry, Rik Mayall and John Sessions; and When I Was a Girl I Used to Scream and Shout starring Julie Walters and Geraldine James.

The Theatre of Comedy Company
(Co-Producer)
The Theatre of Comedy Company Limited, which was formed by Ray Cooney in 1983 with some 30 actors and writers, has produced a wide variety of productions since its first smash hit with Ray Cooney's Run for Your Wife way back in 1983. They include Peter O'Toole in Shaw's Pygmalion, Alan Ayckbourn's marathon two-hander sequence Intimate Exchanges, See How They Run (winning Founder-Member Maureen Lipman an Olivier Award), Peter Nichols's Passion Play and Priestley's When We Are Married (winning Olivier Awards for Best Comedy Performance - Bill Fraser - and Best Comedy Production). After a period of concentration on the refurbishment of the Shaftesbury (of which the Company owns the freehold), the Company returned to active production in splendid style with Ray Cooney's Out of Order, which won the Olivier Comedy of the Year Award for 1991. This production had a long and successful tour.

The Company's recent West End productions have been John Guare's Six Degrees of Separation (in a co-production with the Royal Court) which won the Olivier Award for the Best Play of 1993 and the critically acclaimed Hay Fever at the Albery Theatre. They also produced a successful tour of John Godber's Happy Families. The Company has collaborated several times with the Royal Court, including the first production of Hysteria. The Company's most recent production was The Prime of Miss Jean Brodie starring Patricia Hodge at the Strand Theatre. Recently the Company took over the management of the Churchill, Bromley and a recent production of Hot Mikado transferred to the Queen's Theatre.

The Company co-produces the very popular TV series As Time Goes By starring founder members Dame Judi Dench and Geoffrey Palmer. The Company also co-produced a new four part series Love on a Branch Line which was screened in June 1994 on BBC TV.

N. CHARLESWORTH 1990

The Duke of York's Theatre

The theatre, which opened on 10 September 1892 with The Wedding Eve, was built for Frank Wyatt and his wife, Violet Melnotte. Initially called the Trafalgar Square, the name was shortened to Trafalgar in 1894, and the following year became the Duke of York's to honour the future King George V. Violet Melnotte owned the theatre for the rest of her life, often leasing it to other managements, mostly - notably in its early history - to Charles Frohman. The first long run under his aegis was Anthony Hope's The Adventures of Lady Ursula. In 1900 Jerome K Jerome's Miss Hobbs was staged on the same bill as a one-act play by David Belasco, a friend of Frohman's. It was entitled Madame Butterfly and, purely by chance, was seen by Puccini who later turned it into what is probably his most famous opera; as such it was ultimately performed at the Duke of York's in 1932 by the Carl Rosa Opera Company.

The theatre's association with J M Barrie began in 1902 with the presentation of The Admirable Crichton. However, the most endearing production arising from this relationship was Peter Pan, first seen in 1904 and revived every Christmas until 1915. The last of Barrie's important works to have its debut at the Duke of York's was What Every Woman Knows, in 1908.

During Frohman's management period there were occasional limited seasons featuring special guest stars, including Isadora Duncan, Sarah Bernhardt, Yvette Guilbert and Albert Chevalier. From February to June 1910, Frohman put on an ambitious repertory season of ten plays - some revivals, some new. Most noteworthy of the untried productions were Galsworthy's Justice, Granville Barker's The Madras House and Shaw's Misalliance.

After Frohman died in 1915, aboard the torpedoed liner Lusitania, another repertory company, Miss Horniman's from the Gaiety, Manchester, took over for a season which included Hindle Wakes by Stanley Houghton. The big money-spinners of the First World War years were Romance, Daddy Long Legs and The Thirteenth Chair in which Mrs Patrick Campbell played Rosalie La Grange. Two considerable successes of the 1920s were revues: The Punch Bowl and London Calling, the latter largely written by Noël Coward. His Easy Virtue starring Jane Cowl, Joyce Carey and Adrianne Allen attracted full houses during 1926 - although his Home Chat the following year did not. Matheson Lang presented and appeared in a number of dramas towards the end of the decade. These included Jew Süss which gave Peggy Ashcroft her first important role in the West End.

The 1930s brought a number of interesting seasons, amongst them The Carl Rosa Opera Company, Grand Guignol, Nancy Price's People's National Theatre, The Ballet Rambert and the notable appearances of Markova and Dolin which greatly helped to popularise ballet in England. Apart from these, a very successful play in 1931 was John van Druten's London Wall in which John Mills scored a great personal triumph.

During the Second World War Is Your Honeymoon Really Necessary? which opened in 1944 enjoyed a two-year run. Subsequently, a pair of peace-time revues,

One Two Three and Four Five Six, starring Binnie Hale, Sonnie Hale and Bobby Howes, played for over twelve months. In the early 1950s John Clements and Kay Hammond achieved an enormous success with The Happy Marriage. Anouilh's Point of Departure, starring Mai Zetterling and Dirk Bogarde, who gave a widely-acclaimed performance, was also staged during this period and Orson Welles' adaptation of Moby Dick, with Joan Plowright, ran for a limited season in 1955. A year later, Hugh Mills' The House By the Lake, starring Flora Robson, played for over 700 performances.

Notable productions during the 1960s include: the revue One Over the Eight with Kenneth Williams and Sheila Hancock, Frank Marcus' The Killing of Sister George, with Beryl Reid and Eileen Atkins, and Alan Ayckbourn's Relatively Speaking, which starred Celia Johnson, Michael Hordern, Richard Briers and Jennifer Hilary.

The following decade started with a two-and-a-half year run of The Man Most Likely to and ended with two distinguished productions - Half Life which was transferred from the National Theatre with John Gielgud in the leading role, and Clouds which paired Tom Courtenay and Felicity Kendal, previously presented at the Hampstead Theatre Club. During the run of Clouds, Capital Radio purchased the freehold of the Duke of York's from Peter Saunders, its then owner, closing it in May 1979 for complete refurbishment, including the removal of a number of pillars from the auditorium.

On 10 February 1980 there was a reopening Gala in aid of the Combined Theatrical Charities at which fifty stars gave their services in a performance reflecting the history of The Duke of York's.

The first production under the aegis of Capital Radio was Rose starring Glenda Jackson, which played to near-capacity business from February to August 1980. The award-winning Duet For One by Tom Kempinski, with Frances de la Tour and David de Keyser, was followed by other successes, including J P Donleavy's The Beastly Beatitudes of Balthazar B, Donald Sinden and Beryl Reid in The School For Scandal, and Al Pacino's award-winning performance in David Mamet's American Buffalo. Richard Harris' comedy Stepping

Out, directed by Julia Mackenzie, ran for almost three years to be succeeded by the acclaimed revival of Alan Ayckbourn's comedy How the Other Half Loves and Tom Stoppard's Artist Descending a Staircase. In June 1989 Willy Russell's Shirley Valentine opened at the Duke of York's, this time with Hannah Gordon, and ran for over two years. The next production was another one-woman show, Dickens' Women, written by and starring Miriam Margolyes, which transferred from the Hampstead Theatre. Two short seasons brought 1991 to a close; they were Stephen Mallatratt's The Glory in the Garden and Sheridan Morley's Noël and Gertie.

In March 1992 the Duke of York's Theatre was bought from Capital Radio by a consortium whose directors are Sir Eddie Kulukundis OBE, Howard Panter, Peter Beckwith, David Beresford Jones and Robin Guilleret. This coincided with London's hottest ticket - the Royal Court's production of Ariel Dorfman's Death and the Maiden which won awards for both the author and Juliet Stephenson's electrifying performance. Roald Dahl's The Witches followed for a highly successful Christmas season.

The Young Vic's production of Arthur Miller's The Last Yankee transferred in 1993 to great acclaim. The Royal Court followed, in September, with another sell-out season. This time it was David Mamet's Oleanna, starring David Suchet and Lia Williams, which took us into June 1994. A long hot summer was made even hotter by Richard O'Brien's The Rocky Horror Show making a pit stop on its 21st Birthday celebratory national tour - tickets were like gold dust. A season with award-winning playwright Jonathan Harvey's Beautiful Thing and a transfer from the National Theatre of Arthur Miller's latest, award-winning play, Broken Glass, brought us back to The Rocky Horror Show in May 1995.

Assistance in the preparation of this article is gratefully acknowledged to Geoffrey Ashton's History of the Duke of York's Theatre.

How the Royal Court is brought to you

The English Stage Company at the Royal Court Theatre is supported financially by a wide range of public bodies and private companies, as well as its own trading activities. The theatre receives its principal funding from the **Arts Council of England,** which has supported the Royal Court since 1956. **The Royal Borough of Kensington & Chelsea** gives an annual grant to the Royal Court Young People's Theatre and provides some of its staff. The **London Boroughs Grants Committee** contributes to the cost of productions in the Theatre Upstairs.

Other parts of the Royal Court's activities are made possible by business sponsorships. Several of these sponsors have made a long term commitment. 1995 saw the fifth Barclays New Stages Festival of Independent Theatre, which has been supported throughout by **Barclays Bank.** **British Gas North Thames** supported three years of the Royal Court's Education Programme. Sponsorship by **WH Smith** helped make the launch of the Friends of the Royal Court scheme so successful.

1993 saw the start of our association with the **Audrey Skirball-Kenis Theatre,** of Los Angeles. The Skirball Foundation is funding a Playwrights Programme at the Royal Court. Exchange visits for writers between Britain and the USA complement the greatly increased programme of readings and workshops which have fortified the Royal Court's capability to develop new plays.

The much expanded season in the Theatre Upstairs by young new writers would not have been possible without the generous sponsorship of **The Jerwood Foundation.** The season was produced in association with the **Royal National Theatre Studio.**

In 1988 the Royal Court launched the **Olivier Building Appeal** to raise funds to restore, repair and improve the theatre building. So far nearly £750,000 has been raised. The theatre has new bars and front of house areas, new roofs, air conditioning and central heating boilers, a rehearsal room and a completely restored and cleaned facade. This would not have been possible without a very large number of generous supporters and significant contributions from the **Theatres' Restoration Fund,** the **Rayne Foundation,** the **Foundation for Sport and the Arts** and the **Arts Council's Incentive Funding Scheme.**

The Royal Court earns the rest of the money it needs to operate from the Box Office, from other trading and from the transfers of plays such as *Death and the Maiden*, *Six Degrees of Separation*, *Oleanna* and *My Night With Reg* to the West End. But without public subsidy it would close immediately and its unique place in British Theatre would be lost. If you care about the future of arts in this country, please write to your MP and say so.

The English Stage Company at the Royal Court Theatre

The English Stage Company was formed to bring serious writing back to the stage. The Court's first Artistic Director, George Devine, wanted to create a vital and popular theatre. He encouraged new writing that explored subjects drawn from contemporary life as well as pursuing European plays and forgotten classics. When John Osborne's *Look Back in Anger* was first produced in 1956, it forced British Theatre into the modern age. But, the Court was much more than a home for 'Angry Young Men' illustrated by a repertoire that stretched from Brecht to Ionesco, by way of J P Sartre, Marguerite Duras, Wedekind and Beckett.

The ambition to discover new work which was challenging, innovative and also of the highest quality became the fulcrum of the Company's work. Early Court writers included Arnold Wesker, John Arden, David Storey, Ann Jellicoe, N F Simpson and Edward Bond. They were followed by a generation of writers led by David Hare and Howard Brenton, and in more recent years, celebrated house writers have included Caryl Churchill, Timberlake Wertenbaker, Robert Holman and Jim Cartwright. Many of their plays are now regarded as modern classics.

In line with the policy of nurturing new writing, the Theatre Upstairs has mainly been seen as a place for exploration and experiment, where writers learn and develop their skills prior to the demands of the Theatre Downstairs. Anne Devlin, Andrea Dunbar, Sarah Daniels, Jim Cartwright, Clare McIntyre, Winsome Pinnock, and more recently Martin Crimp and Phyllis Nagy have benefited from this process. Theatre Upstairs productions have regularly transferred to the Theatre Downstairs, as with Ariel Dorfman's *Death and the Maiden*, and this autumn Sebastian Barry's *The Steward of Christendom*. The latter was part of a major season of plays by writers new to the Royal Court, many of them first plays, produced in association with the **Royal National Theatre Studio** with sponsorship from **The Jerwood Foundation**. The writers included Joe Penhall, Nick Grosso, Judy Upton, Sarah Kane, Michael Wynne, Judith Johnson and James Stock.

1992-1994 were record-breaking years at the box-office with capacity houses for productions of *Faith Healer*, *Death and the Maiden*, *Six Degrees of Separation*, *King Lear*, *Oleanna*, *Hysteria*, *Cavalcaders*, *The Kitchen*, *The Queen & I* and *The Libertine*. *Death and the Maiden* and *Six Degrees of Separation* won the Olivier Award for Best Play in 1992 and 1993 respectively. *Hysteria* won 1994's Olivier Award for Best Comedy, and also the Writer's Guild Award for Best West End Play. *My Night with Reg* won the 1994 Writer's Guild Award for Best Fringe Play, the Evening Standard Award for Best Comedy, and Best Comedy in this year's Olivier Awards. Jonathan Harvey won the 1994 Evening Standard Drama Award for Most Promising Playwright, for *Babies*.

After nearly four decades, the Royal Court's aims remain consistent with those established by George Devine.

The Royal Court Theatre is still a major focus in the country for the production of new work. Scores of plays first seen in Sloane Square are now part of the national and international dramatic repertoire.

Rat in the Skull

Rat in the Skull was first staged at the Royal Court Theatre, London, on 31 August 1984, with the following cast:

Superintendent Harris	Philip Jackson
PC Naylor	Gary Oldman
Detective Inspector Nelson	Brian Cox
Roche	Colum Convey

Directed by Max Stafford-Clark
Designed by Peter Hartwell

From black an overhead screen shows clinical photographs of facial and trunk injuries to **Roche**, *taken head on and in profile.*

We end on a shot of his face with split eye, nose and lip.

Roche *strolls under the screen.*

He smokes a cigarette hooked under his palm, jail-bird and corner-boy style.

His testimony is measured, sly, almost humorous.

Roche   The holiday snaps.

Dear Mum, this is me in London Town. I've seen all the sights, the Tower, the Zoo, McDonald's and the bottom sides of coppers' boots from the wrong way up.

They showed me the doings. I was sat on my hunkers, minding my own business, wondering whether to pick my nose or go for a slash and a sledge-hammer comes through the door, without so much as by your leave. Followed in short order by half a dozen of the larger size of bobby, waving guns and shouting hallo.

One of them shakes me by the balls and throws me across the room before I've a chance to say I didn't catch the name and I'm not that inclined even so, and then it's down the stairs, the Human Brick and into the Paddy Wagon, through the black arse end of which many a good man before yours truly has found himself, and never a reason given him neither.

Then in comes the massed bands of the Metropolitan Police shouting hallo again, to sit on my head by way of keeping me company to Paddington Green, and could you ask for a nicer nick, five stars and crossed truncheons. They grow these London coppers big, believe me. They like them big and ugly.

But fair play – never a hand on me after the arrest. The violence of the tongue, yes, and excited waving of the shooters but nothing more than that except the odd gag about why don't we save the taxpayer the cost of keeping the sod the rest of his natural and heave him arse over tit out of the back of the van?

But they meant no harm by it. What's new about taking the rise out of a poor bewildered Paddy? A bit of sport. Great crack. Not a hand on me. Not even the hand of the one who lost a brother to a brick in Derry in seventy-two.

Mind you, he turns a worrying shade of green when I say as soon as I'm back home I'll look up the hand of the man that threw the brick and shake it hard. But that was just my bit of sport. My crack. He knew I meant no harm by it – though it did take six of them to keep him off your loving son, Michael Patrick de Valera Demon Bomber Roche.

Superintendent Harris *enters, in civilian clothes, wary, alert and pissed off.*

Harris   Fetch me the cell-block register, the medical report, the statements of the arresting, receiving and processing officers, notebooks of the same and the bollocks of the cell-block duty officer, lightly fried.

One phone call to my missis, with apologies, the switchboard to log all calls out, the hard word put round if news of what happened to the Irishman this afternoon gets about outside this station it's goolie kebabs all around.

The little slip of a thing who hasn't popped his cherry yet, who still hasn't got hairs on it, who found Paddy in that condition together with all the paperwork going back to the Dead Sea Scrolls, including the original fucking blueprints for fucking Noah's fucking ark.

He waits, surveying the blow-up of the injuries as **Roche** *speaks again in the same tone.*

Roche   Not a hand on me. For the next two days, not a hand on me.

Heavy verbals, oh ay – they must have been running buses, there was coppers coming in from all over the place, they were that proud of me, Michael Patrick de Valera Demon Bomber Roche. Privacy be damned with formation teams of interrogators coming in every hour, on the hour, Hard Man

Soft Man, like a smack in the gob, son? Like a fag or a
woman? Relays, rakes and queues of the bastards and as one
falls dead with exhaustion it's out by the legs and the next
man please.

The barking at you and showing you snaps of bits and pieces
of what was left of the poor buggers when the things went up
and hanging's too good and the cell light left on all the time
and peering up your backside with the Everready and
breakfast a mug of cold tea the copper said he'd gobbed in
and every time when you were left alone whoever walked by
the cell door aimed a kick at it for badness.

But I gave them nothing. The Human Clam, me. I mean, I
was nothing like the poster. I'm no oil painting God knows
but you have your pride. Not a note from me, though damn
all good that would have done, me with the stuff under my
bunk and the forensic coming in any day.

I was saying nothing and never a hand on me but fair play,
this Mick, far away from home, was stitched up solid and the
cops were playing it by the book and down the line and not a
foot put wrong and I'm telling you there were twenty-five to
life big black ones sure-fire thing coming up.

The world was turning into iron bars for yours truly,
Michael Patrick de Valera You-Know-The-Rest-Of-It
Roche.

Harris   Naylor?

PC Naylor *steps forward into the spill of light, nervous, knowing
he's in big trouble.*

Naylor   Sir?

Harris   Son, the Giant Turd From Outer Space is just
about to come hurtling through the ionosphere and hit you
in the back of your shiny neck. All over this nick notebooks
are being scribbled up, diaries and day books being
rewritten, the smart and hairy arsed are putting daylight
between themselves and what happened to the Irishman this
afternoon.

You can't put daylight between yourself and that unfortunate event. You were there. It looks to me that Naylor the cherry goes down with the other fella on it.

You hit the prisoner?

Naylor　No sir.

Harris　The other fella hit him, you hit him.

Naylor　I wasn't in the cell when the incident took place, sir.

Harris　But you should have been.

Naylor　Sir.

Harris　Standing orders.

Naylor　Sir.

Harris　No officer from the Royal Ulster Constabulary will remain unsupervised with an Irish prisoner, from north or south of that bloody border, not while we have custody. What our friends from the RUC get up to when they're back home is up to them, known only to the Great Paddy In The Sky. Here, on our turf, we ride shotgun.

You step sideways to dodge the Giant Turd From Outer Space on the assault charge by wittily saying you wasn't in the cells when the incident took place – dear oh dear – the Turd Comet From Mars gets you right on the nose.

Naylor　I never hit him, sir. I was not in the cell when the alleged incident took place. I have no statement to make unless this is a formal disciplinary hearing in which case I should like a representative from the Federation to be present.

Sir.

Harris　Hark at the babby. Who put you up to that? Some beery flatfoot in the canteen with twenty-five years in of pounding the beat? Take no notice son. I say you want to take no notice. This is you and your daddy –

Naylor (*to himself, wearily*)　Mornings I wish I had not got out of bed –

Harris   – who's trying to find out what went on and plug what holes we can. Buy that? Better you had. This morning they had one Hibernian here in mint condition.

Now that man looks like he's had major roadworks happen on his face and ribs and one copper's facing a Grievous Bodily Harm and maybe two –

Naylor   Life leave it out –

Harris   Alternative – you left the RUC man alone with a fellow Irishman and he tuned him up with boot and fist and a lot of dangerous and dirty police work, not to mention hard slogging pavement-pounding is going down the drain. Because the courts do not like to think that in this civilised little island confessions are routinely extracted, even from the foreigner with boot, fist or chairleg.

Pause.

Harris   He came in Monday –

Naylor   He did.

Harris   Interview file including first statement, ultimately withdrawn –

*He turns as **Naylor** proffers him a file. As he studies it, **Roche** speaks. For the first time he looks a little uneasy, his cockiness dented –*

Roche   I'm not denying I gave them a statement.

By the Friday, the state I was in, I'd have given them anything, like many a better man before me.

You've no idea if it's day or night, if you're coming or going and you'd sell your granny to a black just to have that cell light out an hour or so – and lift him on to her if you could get your head down for the night without coppers tap dancing on your door.

It's in the book. Stick it while you can, then give them what they want. They leave you alone while they're typing it up and colloguing with the others and buying each other drinks on the strength of having cracked you. Meanwhile you're having your bit of shut-eye and when they come breezing back you deny you ever saw the thing with your name on it.

It's in the book. It's the name of the game. Haven't us and the boys in blue been at it long enough, since the Fenians a hundred years and more back?

I gave them the buggering statement. And then I took it back. And then, as you might say, the long night wore on.

Harris *finds the statement in the files.*

Harris   Pathetic. You ever need a brain transplant, Constable Naylor, and they give you the choice between a Nobel prize-winner and an Irishman, take the Irishman's. Ten to one it's hardly been used.

Roche   Paddy's got wise and Paddy's got smart. He's got the book on them by now –

Harris   He takes the statement back and the boys have to start feeding him through the meat grinder all over again. But this time they know they can crack him and he knows it too.

Roche   And how the hell shouldn't Paddy know the stink of them by now? Haven't us and them been playing tag with hatchets long enough? You think I just got off the boat? –

Harris (*checking the file*)   They crack him again. At three in the morning, Sunday. Second statement. Half as long again as the first. Singing his cotton socks off. Then he gets his second wind and takes it back again.

Roche   Who better than sly old Paddy to lead the cops a dance? –

Harris   And Sunday night he signs it. That's his mark. Gotcha.

Roche   I'm not denying I signed a statement, the state I was in –

He stops.

Roche   That cell light's a crippler, right enough and what the hell? There was enough stuff under my bunk to move Buckingham Palace a half mile up the road with Tin Lizzy and Phil the Greek inside it.

He stops again.

Roche   Anything to get the bastards off me and get my head down. Forgive me Father, for I have coughed. The confessional urge. A thousand Sundays muttering into the God Box. Forgive me Father. And who's to say there's no taking it back? First thing Monday, free of the God Box for another week?

And isn't there something fine and grand and flying high about saying Yes, you've got your man, you're on the ball right enough, this is Michael Patrick de Valera Demon Bomber Roche present and correct?

Forgive me Father, those brave lads in blue will never get it through their inch-thick Anglo-Saxon skulls there'll be a dozen after me and a dozen more. They never understood Paddy when they had him by the balls and they don't understand him now, when he's got them by theirs.

I'll sign and Up the Rebs.

Harris   Gotcha, my son.

He folds the file.

Harris   They went fifteen rounds with him and got the win on points. Fished him, hooked him, played him, gaffed him. His only way out, maybe, is something like a deal.

Naylor   A deal, sir?

Harris   Think on.

Gotcha. He's sat on the spike and looking for a way off if only offered in the right way. Only human. These fellas are you and me, Naylor, they cough and spit and scratch their pills and any way out of twenty-five, even twenty-five for old Mother Ireland, the wrong side of the pond.

Naylor   Getting heavy, this, sir.

Harris   Too true. True word.

Naylor   But I shouldn't bring my rep in yet, you say?

Harris   You and your daddy, this.

Naylor   It's not even my station, the Green.

(*Getting no help for the moment.*) It could be, this officer from Belfast was going to turn him?

Harris   I think the word is convert, Constable Naylor. Fitting usual, you might think.

Naylor   Sir?

Harris   Convert? The term theological?

Naylor (*still not understanding*)   Oh –

Harris   Her Majesty's Government has approved the policy of obtaining convictions in these difficult times on the word of informers, converted terrorists struck by remorse at their past misdeeds, mindful that they might get early parole in exchange, suitcases of money. He was being looked at. The hint was there. The bid was in.

All was needed was someone who specialised in that mucky side of things to check his profile.

Naylor   Detective Inspector Nelson –

Harris   Royal Ulster Constabulary. A specialist.

Now you know what he was doing here. And what you were meant to be doing just by your presence in the cell was making sure our visiting colleague didn't go for a walking holiday all over that profile. Instead of which I believe you went for a cuppa. Was having a dish of tea leaving two Irishmen alone to tear each other's ears off for use as oven gloves.

Roche *speaks with cockiness returned.*

Roche   I said I wouldn't see him.

Nelson *can be seen, with overcoat and flight bag, waiting, half lit.*

Roche   I says Copper I'm taking no more calls, especially not from a member of Northern Ireland's Royal Ugly Constabulary. No way. I'd a pal come out of Castlereagh Interrogation Centre with a burst spleen. My dad had his head split open by an RUC baton; thanks, we already gave.

I says the only way I want to see a member of Her Imperial Majesty's Royal Orange Constabulary is down the hairs of

an Armalite cross-sight. I says the only way I'm going to talk
to one is through a medium. And so on. Mick the Lip.

But it's funny what you get used to, isn't it? They left me
alone to think it over and wasn't I beginning to miss red-
faced cops yelling at me all the time? And I thought, I know
your game, I know what you're after.

I'll go along for the ride. I'll have a twopenny one. Just to
clock the face in the hopes one day I'll be squinting at it
down the barrel. Just to see how they work the informer
ramp.

I swear to God that's all it was. A deal never crossed my
mind. I put my hand on the jumping bleeding heart of Jesus
and I say that's all there was to it.

Stops.

Roche   It was the scowling Mick versus the Royal Orange
Gorilla.

The lights black on **Roche**.

Harris (*to* **Naylor**)   I've had Paddy up to here and that's a
fact. Maybe I've been this side of things too long, I've seen
too many. And that goes for the good guys too, the Nelsons
as well as the Roches. Scratch them and they're all Paddies
underneath.

I don't like what they've done to my job of honest coppering.
I don't like *this* –

He indicates the bruised and bloodied face of **Roche** *on the blow-up.*

Naylor   I'm not trying to dump it on someone else but if
the Desk or Cell-Block Duty wised me up –

Harris   Once upon a time there weren't bomb warnings on
the Tube. Once upon a time a pigeon could have a
straightforward crap on a Whitehall window ledge without
having to dodge the bomb-netting. You could get a straight
view of the street without thinking there go the eyes, if the
strange motor badly parked down there gives a big green
puff and goes sixty feet in the air. Once upon a time you
didn't get a pain in the kidneys when they put you in letter-

opening detail; you didn't spend a morning once or twice a year wading ankle-deep through broken glass looking for some poor bleeder's missing foot or head; once upon a time coppering was coppering; bombs was what wogs threw at each other, never white men; Paddy liked his pint and the only bother he ever gave was having to be bounced out of the bar come Saturday night. Once upon a time.

Naylor   No way I'm trying to dump it. I'm admitting I left the two of them in the cell but if the Desk had said, if the Cell-Block Duty Officer had said –

Harris   Ain't no way you're going to dump it, my little cherry, on the Desk or cell-block wally, whatever that beery flatfoot's been belching in your ear – forget all thoughts.

Naylor *decides to cross the bridge.*

Naylor   Any chance of a bit of help here, sir? The Green ain't my station, I don't know anyone here. I've got my two-year board coming up next month.

Could anything be done?

Harris   If you could sort out your loyalties, PC Naylor, I should see if anything could be done, I should. Your dear old daddy might be able to give you a pointer or two. If you help him.

Naylor   Not my nick, two-year board, I'm spitting feathers and that's straight up.

Harris   Maybe something could be stitched up for you, if we kept the Federation and who knows who else out of it – because I have my loyalties sorted.

Like for you. I object to foreign coppers coming here and screwing up for our lads. Especially the trusting little cherries like yourself, who hasn't hairs on it, still in his probationary. Trusting little babs, taken cruel advantage of by foreign cops. I object to that. I *object.*

The lights black on **Harris.**

Nelson *looks at the screen showing the injuries to* **Roche.**

Nelson   Belfast-bound or Belfast-been you're set apart. Cut out from the other arrivals and departures. Corralled off. Unclean. Infected. Bearing madness, sweating sin.

Oh yes, no doubt about it, that's my work all right. The old one-two. That big farmer's fist, straight from the shoulder. The jab in the gob and a cross to the blinker. My work and no mistake. Want me to sign it? Unclean.

Naylor (*to* **Nelson**)   The prisoner says he doesn't want to see you, after all. Too bad I said.

Nelson   I'm not thrilled skinny to be seeing him. I'm supposed to be on leave.

Naylor   I wouldn't have thought you fellas drew leave.

Nelson   We get away now and then. Majorca last time. It pissed down the whole two weeks.

Naylor   There's the overtime, though.

Nelson   Oh yes indeed, there's the overtime.

Naylor   Accommodation sorted?

Nelson   Thanks.

Naylor (*hands him files*)   Are you going straight in or do you want to go through that first?

Nelson   I'll see him now.

Naylor   Once you've seen one, you've seen them all, eh?

Nelson (*elsewhere*)   What?

Naylor   The file –

Nelson   Oh yes. There's only two sorts of Northern Irishman. The farmers' sons and the city rats.

Naylor   I've got a mate with your mob. Reckoned London coppering was dull, wanted to see the sharp end, said it would look good on his sheet in a couple of years' time.

Nelson   It'll look all right on the headstone as well. Wouldn't you say? 'He saw the sharp end.'

Naylor (*unsure*)   No. You never think of you lot getting leave somehow. Having days off. Doing the ordinary coppering things.

Nelson (*warning*)   You're giving me the second look.

Naylor   Sir?

Nelson   We fart and cough and like our beer, like the rest of you. We're coppers busy coppering, just like you, in the real world. (*Hands him his case.*) Look after the bag.

Is he saying anything?

Naylor   Not now. Not since they okayed you to see him.

Nelson   Were you in when he signed?

Naylor   I've just come on, sir, detailed to you.

Nelson   And what sort's he, would you say? Having seen me, the farmer's son. What sort's Roche?

Naylor   City rat, sir and no mistake. (*Hesitation.*) He's not pleased you're here.

Nelson   He's not?

Naylor   There's been no violence yet – but he's cooking.

Nelson   So let's give him a shake –

The lights switch up on **Roche**, *waiting for the interrogation.*
Naylor *sits as* **Nelson** *takes his time surveying* **Roche**.

Nelson   Pulled back from leave, for this. For you.

Why bother, I said? Your man has coughed fifteen pages, you have his name on it. He'll go back on it, sure, shout rape and blue murder when the trial date's fixed, how they booted it out of him. But that won't wash – (*Flipping through the file.*) A medical check after every interview, not a mark on you. Though that won't stop you trying. Will it? (*Waiting.*) And there he'll sit, the Human Clam. Tight as the fundament of the shark at several atmospheres. Saying nothing, least of all to a gorilla from the RUC.

(*At* **Naylor**.) What did he say when they told him I was flying in? Nothing doing? The only way he'll speak to an

RUC man is through a medium? Give him two thousand foot of wire and a ton of high explosive, he might say yes?

(*Back towards* **Roche**.) And you know and I know, between you and me and the cell door, there's no real point to me digging into you about events and characters back home, is there?

These boys aren't going to let you home in a hurry. They pulled you in, they're going to keep you. Whatever you might have been up to back in Belfast, it's more important that you get done for breaking a few shop windows in Oxford Street or disturbing the traffic in Horse Guards Parade.

Name of the game. *Nom de jouer.*

So I've had my leave wrecked for bugger all and you're missing out on shuteye for likewise. You'll just sit there, playing with your papist prick –

(*Waiting.*) Sorry. Crude, that. The kind of thing you'd expect from a cop. But I'm not here as a cop, am I? Because you said you wouldn't see one – not from back home anyway. So if I'm here at all, I'll just be another fella from the quare old place, God love it, looking for a wee bit of crack with a fellow countryman –

(*As if puzzled, to* **Naylor**.) But now we have a problem. Your man here denies the existence – note – the existence, not just the right to exist but the established fact, the stub-your-toe-on-the-concrete reality that there is such a place as –

Holy Moley – we can't even agree on a name for what we're fighting about. Ulster? The Six Counties? The North-East? The Bloody North? (*Shrugs.*) Forget that for now, let's just say I'm another brand of Irishman.

And then again – how could a mongrel dog like me ever claim that proud name, answering in a confusing sort of way to being half of everything and nothing much of anything – Scots Irish, Irish Scots, but ever just the one and certain fact, one thing for sure in the entire bloody boiling – no way straight Irish on the rocks? (*A sigh.*) So I'm here as a copper after all. We can hang on to that.

(*Back to* **Roche**.) I'm a cop and you're a poor unfortunate sod found with enough how's-your-father under your bunk to send you into orbit if you smoked in bed.

Copper and con. (*Slaps his forehead*.) Jumping Jehosophat – that doesn't work either, does it? Because there's a war on and I'm a collaborator with the Army of Occupation – a traitor working for the Brits in a colonial war, so the normal rules don't apply. (*Relaxing*.) So why don't we say, this is just fellas, from somewhere around the same neck of the woods, having a wee chat about nothing in particular. (*Beat*.) Except the one fella isn't going to say a word to the other because the one fella says the only time he's pleased at the sight of an RUC man is when he's in that pine box and his cap neatly on top of it and a lot of people walking behind it crying their eyes out and I've seen that many a time the past few years, too many –

(*Alert, waiting for a response*.) Were you going to say something? You've followed a lifetime of coffins down your narrow streets and all?   .

I'm sure you have. So that's something we have in common. But not enough for the purposes of conversation, polite or otherwise, I see. Your lips are sealed.

(*Closer to* **Roche**.) I'm going to break you, son. Come the end of the day I'll have you because I am one pissed-off cop who's had his leave wrecked for you and I will get inside you, pal, I will get behind your eyeballs and your lungs, I will wear your ears and nipples, I will feel your swinging, banging balls between my legs and I will hear you say –

(*Stopping suddenly, a smile to* **Naylor**.) I wouldn't mind a cup of tea. Two. One for me and one for Roche here.

Naylor   Two teas sir, yes sir.

Nelson   A cuppa the colour of tar and tasting much the same. Tea, as the saying goes, you could trot a mouse on. And stint not with the sugar.

(*As* **Naylor** *doesn't move*.) What's this? Still life with truncheon? Two teas, miss. Three, if you're choking too.

Naylor   Beg pardon sir, standing orders, cell-block interview wing, sir. None of the Paddies are to be left unsupervised. One uniformed officer to be present at all times for the protection of the interviewing officer.

Nelson   The animal bites, does it?

Naylor   More protection from complaints. Oppressive treatment, victimisation.

Nelson   Does this apply to all interviewing officers from visiting forces or just those from Belfast and environs?

Naylor (*flustered*)   I couldn't say sir. All sir. I don't know, sir. See, this isn't my home station. There was a shout for someone to stand in –

Nelson (*turning away from him, towards* **Roche**)   You want a cup of tea, my friend, you ask me for it. You hear that? You ask me and I'll toe his backside for it, whatever standing orders say.

(*Back to* **Naylor**.) And if I ever hear you refer to this man again as Paddy, I'll get annoyed. Vexed. Miffed. Raging. Understand?

Naylor   Sir.

Nelson   Likewise Mickey, Taig or Fenian Bastard.

Naylor   Sir –

Nelson   Even if he is a Mickey, Taig or Fenian Bastard, because each one of those has a shade of meaning a cockney like yourself is not capable of understanding. Each a particular conjugation in the grammar of hate, as my missis would say. A precise inflection. As she might say and often has.

Married man?

Naylor   No sir, courting.

Nelson   Too lazy to wank, eh?

Naylor   Sir?

Nelson   How about your pal, looking to see the sharp end over there?

Naylor   He'll be leaving that till after, I should think.

Nelson   Wise man.

What's in it for the missis, after all, waiting for the knock on the door, the hard word that Roche and pals have qualified her for the widow's pension?

It's them ought to get the medals when they're being handed out. Although there's some compensation in the grand departmental funeral. They do you a class send-off and the missis gets to star. Queen for a day. All the cameras on her as her legs go under her outside the church, with the kiddies leaning against her, crying buckets or trying to be brave wee men.

Any kids?

Naylor   No sir. Not married sir. Courting.

Nelson   Roche? Do you have parental responsibilities? As well as explosive?

Waits, but gets no answer to his sudden question.

Nelson   Your lot do you a good send-off and all, don't they? I have to hand you that.

The grieving widow, the staring kids and the grim-faced brothers. The trick's to get a slack news night, or else they stick you in between the kitten-stuck-up-a-tree story and the weatherman and where's the dignity in that after all you've done for Queen and Country – or to them?

No kiddies, Roche? No cup of tay? Are you not addicted, then, to the other of the national vices? Do you go along with murder but draw the line at tea drinking?

Well, you might have a point – when you think of all the death and destruction planned across those endless cups of tay in all those little back kitchens where the light never gets in down all those slum backstreets in your home town and mine, it makes you wonder what they put in the stuff –

(*Closer to him, threatening again.*) You'll ask me for that cup of tea. Before we're done, you'll yes sir me and no sir me and can I have that cup of tea please sir and we'll play it how it used to be, the Orange boot on your unwashed Roman neck. I know you, Demon Bomber Roche, down to the soggy skin between your unwashed Fenian toes, like you think you know me. (*Quickly.*) You like that, do you? Demon Bomber Roche? Hint of a grin there, was there? Did you bite? (*Waits.*) Maybe not.

(*Relaxing, pulling away again.*) Roche the Clam. Twenty-five brothers and sisters living in a two-bedroom lean-to in Rickett City along the Falls. His dear old granny going on the Pill at ninety having done her bit to breed the Proddies out.

(*At **Naylor**.*) You get the picture?

(*Back to **Roche**, without waiting for an answer.*) Frantic rejoicing at the happy event of his birth, as the old dear's now not only on a thousand pounds a week family allowance but entitled to a colour telly on the rates and a free seat next time the Pope plays an Irish gig.

It goes without saying the family were committed to the Nationalist cause. The old fella, Michael Patrick de Valera Up The Rebels Roche The First had been interned in the thirties forties fifties sixties and seventies and by an administrative error, the eighties too.

He'd seen so much of the Crumlin and the Maze it's a wonder he managed to breed with Roche's ma at all – a failed nun whose idea of a night well spent was to lure little Protestant boys back to her slum and pull their winkies off.

Maybe he managed to do it in the envelope of his weekly letter home, who knows?

Check?

Naylor (*fazed*) Sir?

Nelson Am I right? Is that what it says in the file?

Naylor Yes sir, check sir.

Nelson   It also goes without saying the family were
discriminated against morning, noon and night by those bad
bastards, the Proddie gang.

They were discriminated against in civil rights and conjugal
rights, denied admission to the Civil Service, the Monarchy
and the best jobs in the Gas Board and whenever they
needed to use a public convenience those crafty Proddie
Swine saw to it there was always someone beat them to it, so
they'd have to stand on one Republican leg and screw up
their Fenian faces until a Proddy'd done his business, which
half the time he'd fake.

As a matter of fact, if ever a one came home and hadn't been
discriminated against they'd fire off a letter of complaint.
They were entitled to abuse. No one ever had it as bad as
them. Don't talk to me of the Nazis and the Jews. What was
done to the niggers or the Red Indians wasn't a patch on it.
(*To* **Naylor**.) Word for word?

Naylor   Word for word.

Nelson   And at nights, as the armoured cars prowled and
the streets hummed with rubber bullets, the Roche clan
would sit round the old peat fire under the autographed
photo of the Holy Father, Polish Pete, playing the tin whistle
and thinking how different it would all be the day old
Ireland dear was free and one.

Mind you, on dole days and family allowance days and when
they wanted a new flat they weren't quite so keen and even
they can see the boys in Dublin have been dragging their feet
about picking up that kind of tab. Breathe a peep of that,
however, and you'd be facing six months in a dentist's chair.

Ignorance. You can't beat it for making you feel all warm
and cosy and snuggled up inside. Tell me the old old stories,
whatever lying side of the line you are.

(*Back at* **Roche**.) On leaving school young Roche, by now a
strapping young consumptive of seven stone and well
recovered from the rickets, has to decide on a career. So
what's it to be – Priest or gunman? Gunman or priest?

(*At* **Naylor** *again.*) The hours are better in the gunman line and there's the Sunday off to think about, and after all there's a tradition in the family, is there not?

Naylor   Sir?

Nelson   Does it not say in there that Roche's family have been blowing up innocent passers-by and cops like me in every generation since the Flood and who's he to buck the trend and let his grey-haired mother down?

Mind you, there's no pension in the gunman line and you're out all hours. Then there's the love life to think about. The skinny blonde with the big knockers and come-hither eyes might turn out to be a Para once you get her back to your place, they'll stop at nothing.

All told, with the robes and incense and kinky gear, the priest has far and away a better chance of pulling the birds and he doesn't have to be looking over his shoulder all the time, unless he's noodling the choirboys, too.

Ah, but Roche, like all his sort, puts women far down the list. He'd rather be running his hand along the barrel of a gun than his own conjugal equipment. He wasn't put on this good earth to breed sons but to kill those of other men so he picks the shooter and off he goes, in a beret two sizes too big and a borrowed pair of dark glasses, with a mother's blessing ringing in his ears, 'Fuck those Orange bastards, son'.

(*Tight in on* **Roche**.) The stuff was under your bunk. Consider.

Getting no response from **Roche**, **Nelson** *turns back to* **Naylor**.

Nelson   An affecting portrait of everyday life down the Falls, Mr Naylor?

Naylor   Word for word.

Nelson   Line for line?

Naylor   Line for line.

Nelson   Look no hands, and I swear I never peeked.

Naylor   You never did sir. Your hands remained attached to your wrists at all times and his file never left my possession.

Nelson   Smart lad. You show a wicked learning curve, son. There must be some Irish in your family somewhere.

Temporary assignment here, you said? Looking to specialise after, are you?

Naylor   You never know, sir.

Nelson   At least it's better than traffic. Can't do any harm watching a specialist at work.

Naylor   Looks good on the sheet, sir, later.

Nelson   I'm sure it will.

Tell me this – aren't you thinking the Irish play it rough with each other? A dirty game?

Naylor   I haven't got my two years in yet, sir. Not for me to comment on another officer's interrogation technique.

Nelson   Interview technique. Interrogation smacks too much of the rubber hose, the wet towel around the face, the sort of thing the word gets around the Paddies get up to between themselves back home. Back home where there's no piece of bum fluff pretending to be a cop riding shotgun, to keep an Anglo eye on things.

Naylor   Yes sir, as I said sir . . . Paddington Green is not my home nick. I'm on assignment, sir, more than volunteer.

Nelson   Not for you to comment, no. Not for you to say it's personal because him and me have followed a thousand coffins down a thousand streets and I know him like he knows me –

(*Stopping suddenly again, lightening the mood.*) Any sign of that cup of tea? Is it still raining?

(*Suddenly back at* **Roche**.) I'm in there, aren't I? Squinting through those piggy Fenian eyes at this RUC gorilla here, this thug of a farmer's son.

One of twenty-seven brothers and all thugs. Brothers, you notice – us Proddies drown the girls at birth. And all of my brothers, it goes without saying, hold down tremendous jobs, and always have done, good jobs with good money, finagled off the papes, we'd none of us feel right in a job unless we pinched it off a Roman with better qualifications for it, somehow. It's that that makes us special.

(*Back at* **Naylor**.) Unlike the runty little Taigs we're good big lads, no rickets for us, ta. Six-footers every one and a fine brave sight we make sat in the back kitchen under the ten foot by ten foot painting of the Queen, God Help Her, putting each other into our uniforms and stuffing the pork chops down our gobs off bone china Coronation Day presentation plates and drinking the tay from mugs showing the Royal Wedding, Charlie, Di and the horse and cart.

There's Sam the Polisman like myself, just come off duty, yanking the broken teeth out of his truncheon. 'Civil rights?' says Sam – 'Wash your mouth out with this' – there's Brother Sam the Ulster Defence Regiment machine-gunner, carving another notch on his gun-butt – God they're hard on litter louts are the UDR – Shaky Sam the Customs Man, stitching another hole in his flak jacket – and slopping the boot black on his face is Holy Terror Sam, Commander-in-Chief, Red Hand of Ulster Counter-Terror Suicide Batallion, hero of a hundred raids. And who's this – it's Sam the Orangeman – well we're all Orangemen, of course, we're born wearing tiny little Orange sashes and the teeniest bowler hats you ever did see, that's how we know to drown the girls –

– but this is Sam *The* Orangeman, Grand Master and Imperial Dragon Of The Celestial Order Of Red-Faced Men In Bowler Hats.

Sam The Orangeman is the fella who actually paints those bloody terrible paintings of his hero, King Billy, on a white horse trampling the papes at the Battle of the Boyne. He's not in the best of health at the moment. He likes a little nip of the hard stuff and Tuesday week mistook the Sinn Fein branch office for the Orange Hall. He was lucky to get away with his life.

As a matter of fact, we're not sure, under all those bandages, if he did get away with his life. If he's not fit for the Twelfth, it's a job for Sam the Undertaker.

You'd be surprised how much call you have for a man like that, when you're all rabid Prods and working for the Crown.

Rabid. There's a word for us. As in devout Catholics, rabid Prods. Bigot. As in Loyalist bigot, staunch Republican.

Where was I?

Naylor (*uncertain*)   Sam the Undertaker? –

Nelson   This year already we've had all the funeral trimmings at a damn good discount on Sam the Magistrate, Sam Sam the Assembly Man, Sam the Preacher and a couple of other Sams who didn't happen to be anyone in particular but just happened to be passing by when one of the brave soldiers for Ireland threw a bomb at the bus queue or into the supermarket.

(*At* **Roche** *again.*) The stuff was under your bunk. Ask a favour.

(*Getting no response, quickly at* **Naylor**.) So you're asking, knowing the odds on an RUC man living to pick up his pension or have enough in the way of arms and legs to stand up and wave without falling over – 'How come, Detective Inspector Nelson, that you signed up?'

Says I, I'll tell you. (*Conspiratorial.*) Sheer blind sectarian hate. Confirm that, Roche? I just wanted to play my part in keeping you bastards down. That's no reason for joining the constabulary, you say, Naylor –

Naylor (*not happy*)   Sir –

Nelson   You joined not just for the bribes from Soho racketeers and East End drug barons but because you wanted to do the simple things, the kindly things, like helping little old ladies across the road. Am I right?

Naylor   I fell for the adverts, sir.

Nelson   You did. Well, let me tell you this – we help little old ladies across the road too. But if we find halfway across they're old ladies of a Catholic persuasion, we leave them there, after hooking their sticks from under them.

That's the sort of bad bastards we are. Isn't that right, Roche? Cup of tay, Roche? Are you ready yet? A half pint of the stuff in a cracked mug, sweet enough to rot your jaw, an oil slick the size of the Med from the greasy spoon stuck in it, a Belfast cup of tay with hairs on it.

(*Still no response, at* **Naylor**.) Comments? Comments on the progress of my interview so far? Any thoughts?

No response from **Naylor**.

Nelson You're right son, keep your distance. Unclean, the pair of us, worth the second look. The one I got from the desk sergeant. The one the briefing officer gave me. The one you're giving me now, that long look cocked down that so superior Anglo-Saxon nose.

This isn't honest coppering, you're right. Is it Rochey? How can it be when every day when I turn out for duty as a walking target I give a polish to my cap badge with my sleeve and what does that cap badge say? – on the one side 'No Surrender' and the other 'Kick the Pope'.

And in my cap band's tucked a slip of paper, the official and unofficial oath of the bulwark of those who will never exchange the blue skies of freedom for the grey mists of an Irish Republic, join in, you know it –

'To the glorious pious and immortal memory of King Billy the Third, who saved us from rogues and roguery, slaves and slavery, knaves and knavery, popes and popery, from brass monkeys and wooden shoes, and whoever denies this toast, all together now, may he be slammed jammed and crammed into the muzzle of the Great Gun of Athlone and the gun fired into the Pope's belly and the Pope into the Devil's belly and the Devil into Hell and the door locked and the key kept in an Orangeman's pocket for ever and may we never lack a brisk Protestant boy to kick the arse of a papist and here's a fart for the Bishop of Cork.'

All, between you and me, big wink, strictly non-sectarian.

Which is why you're stood there between him and me,
Mister Naylor, ever the umpire and sure you couldn't leave
us alone to blink or I'd be down his scrawny Fenian throat or
him down mine.

Goaded, **Roche** *jumps to his feet, fists bunched. The chair goes flying
as* **Nelson** *squares up to him. They freeze as* **Naylor** *speaks
resentfully and regretfully.*

Naylor   Wangle a tour at Paddington Green, where it's
Paddies, whores and A-Rabs?

Pull the other. Volunteer for a high risk nick like this? Riding
shotgun with this fucking madman? Get my backside toed
here, more like. You're on the list Naylor, and you know
what you can do. Yes sarge, No sarge. Specialise? In Anti-
Terror? Pull it again, Pat. I like to get home nights. Cherry I
might be but I'm not signing up for no Holy War. I've seen
how it gets them, even the hard cases like Harris. You've had
Paddy up to here, sir? Seen him one too many? You get the
kick you lying bastard sir, you couldn't do without. You're
turned on by the bomb-proof netting and the broken glass.
You're up the sharp end, where good keen coppers like to be.
Pull the other but leave me out. I'll do my eight and fuck on
off.

They always want to sign you up. They want it to get you
like it's got them. But I don't want to know the ins and outs,
the hows and whys, the back in the mists of bleeding time.
Harris has to try, for all he says he's had it up to here, the
lying bastard. How could he do the job without? See what I
mean? How could you do the job without, you lying bastard
Mr Harris sir? But pally here, no way. Put in my eight and
off I fuck.

But the bastards always sign you up. You're in there with
them every time. Does this make sense? Nelson signs me up.
A double act, the old one-two. Me and him on Roche,
looking for a way to crack him. Straight man, me. Then
something happens and I'm the mark.

Does that make sense? Roche hasn't said a word, the sod.
But now he's straight man to Nelson and I'm the mark. Does

that make sense? Without a word it's him and Roche on me.

Now I'm taking note. This is not routine. This is not per per. Now I'm taking note and figuring the angles, sir. There's something wrong. I'd got a sense that Giant Turd From Outer Space was in orbit around my head, Mr Harris, sir, already, sir.

I'm taking note, I'm figuring the angles. Hoping to Christ the cell-block or desk duty officer would stick their head in. I'm in there with them. They'd signed me up. I'm part of their Holy Fucking War and leave me out, I'd said.

Loyalty sorted. All present and correct, Mr Harris, guv. I'll go into the box against Nelson, I'll do for that Irish bastard, sir.

As he turns back to **Nelson** *and* **Roche**, *they unfreeze, still nose to nose with fists bunched.*

Nelson   Pick that chair up, Mr Naylor.

Naylor   Cell-block duty officer, sir?

Nelson   What for?

Naylor   Assistance sir, your own protection –

Nelson   From this?

Naylor   Allegations sir. Oppressive treatment. Brutality.

Nelson   Pick up that chair. Don't bollix it, not now.

A reluctant **Naylor** *moves to comply.*

Nelson (*at* **Roche**)   You're boxed up, man. There's the one way out.

(*Backing off a little, giving him room.*) There's no walking away for you and me, is there?

Don't you envy the wee lad there? He can do his twenty-five, fuck off, retire and fence stolen goods for a country pub with roses round the door. Me? No matter when I hang up my boots, you boys might come knocking. Up to retirement and past it, every time the front door goes or a foot kicks over a milk bottle in the night, every time I turn my car key like that I'll be thinking now, is it now?

Now is that revolution or even Holy War? I'd say all it was was two fellas in a ditch, clubbing each other till the one dropped dead.

He indicates that **Naylor** *should carefully put the chair back.*

Nelson Easy with that chair now.

I'm not saying Mr Roche has it any easier. He's in his mob for life and all.

(*Closing in on* **Roche** *again.*) You can't afford to doubt, no more than I can. You can't risk letting the rat get in the skull, telling you you're wrong, the fight's not worth the fight and even if it is, why should it be my fight, there are others, I've done my bit, I say no and walk away –

But you can't, no more than I can. Ask me for that cup of tea –

(*Waiting.*) Tell me you never heard it scuttling around between your ears, those long nights on the run hiding up, waiting for the sledge-hammer to come through the door? The rat never said Hey up – what sort of people am I risking my life and liberty and peace of mind for? Just what the hell am I doing up to my neck with the likes of them, that could send that telegram to Hitler?

Roche You what?

Nelson You know what I'm talking about. (*At* **Naylor**.) It went home, see. The rat's been nibbling on that one.

Roche What telegram to Hitler?

Nelson Didn't Eamon de Valera send a telegram to Berlin after Hitler killed himself?

Roche Is that so?

Nelson It's a matter of record.

Roche Are you serious?

Nelson (*shrugging, dismissive*) It's a historical fact.

Roche   And what the hell's it to do with you or me or the price of eggs?

Nelson   They didn't tell you that? They kept that from you? What else, maybe?

Roche   If Eamon de Valera sent a telegram to Hitler –

Nelson   Condolences, more like, on behalf of the Irish Free State.

Roche   That was a little bit before my time and if it mattered either way it still wouldn't matter a damn. If you're so hard up for something to row about – Queen Victoria sent horse blankets in the Famine.

Nelson   So the story goes –

Roche   That's a fact –

Nelson   And you're mad as hell about it.

Roche   I didn't say I was mad as hell.

Nelson   You'd have a right to be – (*At* **Naylor**.) Wouldn't you say? Like I've a right to be mad about that telegram.

Roche   You think there's some comparison?

Nelson   I think it goes to show.

Roche   What?

Nelson   The sort you are.

Roche   The sort that sends telegrams to Hitler? (*At* **Naylor**, *exasperated*.) Get him out of here. I'm being tormented by a eejit.

Nelson   Eejit is it? I'm not the one facing twenty-five to life.

Roche   I'm saying nothing.

Nelson (*sensing he's losing him, turning to* **Naylor**)   Perhaps we'd better explain the term, with an illustrative example.

Mrs Magee's in the butcher's Christmas Eve with only a pound in her purse for a turkey – the old man's been on the booze again and she doesn't want to disappoint the wains.

'Away on, missis' says the butcher, 'a pound? For a turkey? You wouldn't get the leg of a budgie for that.' 'What am I to do?' says she. 'I tell you what' says he – 'I'll skin you a rabbit.' 'A rabbit? For Christmas dinner?' 'The kids won't know the difference.'

He skins it for her and as she's hurrying home with it in her shawl she trips and it falls on the pavement, all pink, with its big ears flopping and its teeth sticking out.

As she's bending over it, carrying on, a drunk steps up and says 'Don't take on missis – sure if it'd lived it'd have been an eejit.'

(*Back to* **Roche**.) I'd say the eejits are the boys like you who've made a bloody balls of everything you put your hand to.

What about the sixties?

Money about, things getting better all the time. A new sort of Proddy who wasn't quite as scared and ignorant as his dad had been in the bad old days. And what happens? Here comes the student mob spouting civil rights and hard in after – the eejits with the shooters.

Roche (*stung*)   So those were the good old days? My dad never had a job in ten years. New flats going up all around, going to the Prods and us sharing a tap with six other families.

Nelson (*appealing to* **Naylor**)   So his daddy opted out of anything but the handouts. His daddy said we can't vote or talk you Proddies into the Free State, we'll bomb and burn you into it instead.

Roche   Nothing. I'm saying nothing.

Nelson   Wasn't there a chance in the twenties? And didn't the eejits blow it then as well?

If they'd stuck to the Treaty their own leaders had signed, the Border would have withered away inside ten years –

Roche (*also turning to* **Naylor**)   Signing that piece of paper was a betrayal of all that the men of 1916 and those of the martyred generations before had fought and died for –

A hundred thousand of his dad and his pals drilling every night and burning whole streets of us out and the voting rigged and the boot on the neck –

Nelson   Because the gun had been out again, down there in Paddy Heaven in the south. The bloodthirsty eejits went to war again, this time with each other and every dead man is another brick in the wall between his dad and mine. And the king eejit, the Yankee de Valera put his almighty conscience on a pole and the littler eejits, who couldn't argue their way to the top of a chip shop queue without a gun in their hands, upped and followed him.

It's no wonder they're crazy on Country and Western down there – they're all cowboys at heart. If it moves, plug it and check the colour of the uniform after.

(*Keeping the initiative.*) I appeal to you, Mr Naylor, as someone not likely to be biased in what must appear to you as far-off tales of long ago –

Naylor   Dead on sir. Could hardly care less, me.

Nelson   Is it likely the North would be desperate to get in bed with the South when they're busy killing each other at a greater rate and with more apparent relish in a civil war than when they were killing the Saxon in the War of Independence?

Naylor   I should think Roche and the rest of them would be very surprised by the amount of time I don't spend trying to make head or tail of it.

Nelson   Come and join the party, we'll wipe the blood off the walls for you. Shift that body off the settee and make yourself at home.

How far back do you want to go?

Naylor   Ninety minutes if you make it quick. A little bit goes a long way with me.

Nelson   Now here's the best Irish joke of the lot – (*At* **Naylor**, *who's gone too far.*) Do you like Irish jokes, Mr Naylor?

Naylor   Side splitters.

Nelson   Nice and simple, aren't they? Do you know why that is?

Naylor   You have me there, sir.

Nelson   So the English can understand them. Say it.

Naylor   So the English can understand them. Very good sir.

Nelson (*turning back to* **Roche**)   The best Irish joke of the lot is if it hadn't been for the likes of you, the eejits with the shooters, England would have dumped the Protestant Embarrassment years back.

But every time the bricks are stacked, along comes the eejits and forget it.

Don't tell me that didn't worry you those long nights, knowing the number one enemy to Dublin and London doing a deal is those shooters you're so fond of waving. Tell me the rat never told you if you want to see the real enemy of United Ireland don't look at me, don't look at Naylor there, or the scared young Jock on patrol in your back yard – just look in the shaving mirror.

Exasperation from **Roche** *as he appeals to* **Naylor** –

Roche   Lock me up. I want locked up. I never asked to see him, I said no way, a gorilla from the RUC –

Nelson   Am I not right? Isn't it you and yours to blame?

Roche   I want out of here now –

Nelson   Put up to it, of course. Taken for a mug by the gang of cheap extortionists and small-time racketeers that pass themselves off as a High Command –

Roche I said only through a medium. I said only down the hairs of an Armalite –

Nelson And where were them fellas when you were sweating it out? Where are they going to be when you're five years into your stretch – six seven, not into double figures yet –

Roche Call the monkey off –

Nelson Eleven twelve – are you counting with me? Fifteen sixteen – and it doesn't make sense beyond that, does it? Where's the point in counting further? Twenty, twenty-one? You can't get your head around it, can you?

Roche *throws his head back, bawling out a song to drown* **Nelson**'s *insistent voice.*

Roche (*sings*)
    Oh then tell me Sean O'Farrell
    Tell me why you hurry so
    Hush ma buachaill hush and listen
    And his cheeks are all aglow
    I bear orders from the Captain
    Get you ready quick and soon –

Nelson It's only the early years you can really understand, five six years, seven, isn't it? And will they all be like each other, or will you look back some time and think, the thirteenth wasn't that bad –

Roche
    For the pikes must be together
    For the rising of the moon –

Nelson – and there were a few laughs all right in the fifteenth. I wonder what the twenties will be like, will there be some good days in them? Am I never getting out, what am I good for when the bastards let me go and where's the fella who put me here?

Roche
    Oh then tell me Sean O'Farrell
    Where the gathering is to be

In the old spot by the river
Right well known to you and me –

Nelson   Wise up man. It's your good luck they sent a smart
monkey across to see you. Take advantage. As a favour.
Swill the stink of this place out with that cup of tea, just you
and me.

Roche   You're good luck, are you? Then I'd hate to meet
your brother. A cup of tay? Just the two of us? A Belfast cup
of tay with hairs on it? I'm far too fly for that one, ta. You
think I just got off the boat? (*At* **Naylor**.) Get this – (*Back to*
Nelson.) You might be dead right, all along. You are a
clever chimp, no one ever said yous didn't have a head on
your shoulders. (*At* **Naylor**.) But I'm a simple soldier, pal,
called up for the duration. Swapping arguments with you is
not my line. That's for others. And even if you could prove to
me the military solution was no solution, that we're a
stumbling block and obstacle to Irish unity and not its
motor, I would still not lay down my arms or agree that a
one of my fellow soldiers should. For taking up a weapon in
the cause of Irish nationhood is not and never has been a
matter of calculation, a cool decision on the odds. If it had
been the flame would not have been lit in every succeeding
generation four hundred years and more –

(*Quietly, almost regretful.*) That's what yous never seem to
understand. It's not the head, it's the heart. Maybe if we lay
low, left it to the chin waggers the troubles would be gone
like snow off a ditch. Maybe we have put our own through
the meat grinder – 'Can we borrow your street for a war,
missis? Do you mind us pulling the town down round your
ears so some day we can build it up again?'

But you nail my hands to the table and I'll still tell you
there's no other way – never was and never will be.

What matters is that there's a job to do and it's just my bad
luck it was me was picked on. And what I had to lay on my
own is nothing compared to what you and yours laid on us.
And say it's no price to pay for the fully free and undivided
national state, sovereign and in possession of every sod and
boulder of our own dear land.

Naylor (*checking his notes, flat, emotionless*)   Me and mine will
not betray the generations of the martyred dead by failure of
resolve or misplaced sentiment or squeamishness because to
pull back now is to condemn the generations yet unborn to
wage this war. Ireland having slumbered for sixty years has
risen to her feet. She never yet again lie down. (*Checks his
notes.*) Will. Will never yet again lie down.

Roche
Our wee school's
A nice wee school
It's made of bricks and mortar
The only thing that's wrong with it's
The baldy-headed master

He goes to church on Sunday
To pray to the Lord
To give him strength
To beat us kids on Monday

Naylor   Concluding with the words –

Roche   Not any longer. No ta. That bastard version of a
state was ripped from Eire's bleeding side by fraud and the
threat of violence. You maintained that banana state by
rigging the voting year in year out and with official violence,
murder and corruption dished out under the heading law
and order. We have you by the throat and England's paper
commitment to her bastard state, which costs her more in
blood and money every year, will likewise be swept away, for
you'll never get us, the risen people, on our knees again.

Naylor   He said. And could he have a sandwich, cheese or
ham.

The lights rise on **Harris**.

Naylor   Notebook entry signed with date place and time,
Morris Brian Naylor, Number MP 752.

Harris   Hefty piece of prose that.

Naylor   First prize short-hand typing training college sir.

Harris   Things I knew and things I didn't know when I got
here two hours back. We'd got a serious assault. That I

knew. I think I know you did as per leave the both of them alone. I don't know why. I want to know because I have to go in there and crack Nelson like he cracked Roche and I am scared of that. I tell you that scares me because I am an ordinary decent copper but forty minutes from here by air you cannot be just that, so can I pull it off? So do not wear me out but tell me how he got you out the room.

Naylor   'Your pilot speaking. We are approaching Belfast Airport. Please set your watches back three hundred years.' (*Pause.*) Joke, sir.

Harris   You just don't want to know the hows and whys do you?

Naylor   Speaking frankly sir, between you and me, sir, on the overall situation, just so we know where we are – I say tow that entire fucking wet island and its incomprehensible bleeding tribes into the Atlantic, pull the plug and give us all some fucking peace and quiet.

Sir.

Harris   You've obviously thought this out in the political as well as the civil engineering detail. However, some of us have to try.

Naylor   Well you chose the specialisation, I take it sir. I say put in your eight and clear on off. I walk on by, I do. Brain sweat about the Paddies? Keep it straight and simple son, the Wise Man said to me, you walk on by.

Harris (*wearily*)   I said do not wear me out. I said how did he get you out the room?

Naylor   *Them* sir. The both of them. How did the two of them get me out of the room?

*Lights up on **Roche** and **Nelson**, who sits on the end of the interview room desk.*

Nelson   Got that off your chest? The obbligato for wind and spittle, as my missis would have called it. And often did. When I laid into it. From a different point of view, of course. Usually after burying a mate. Following one of those coffins

with the cap on it. Or being honour guard, if I knew the
fella.

I usually knew the face at least. It's not all that big a ditch
we're fighting in and for. Maybe I'd be riding shotgun on the
hearse, because we don't even let each other bury our dead
in peace, do we? It's not enough just to have clubbed the
bastard dead.

(*Beat.*) That cup of tea, now you've said your piece? Don't
tell me you're just a simple soldier, Roche. You blow the
arms and legs off the language too. You torture the meaning
of things, like you've cut into every part of us that thinks or
feels.

'Active service units – simple soldiers – execution –
collaboration' – How sick I am of your cheap and easy
rhetoric and how easy it is for you to grab the monopoly of
love for Ireland, while you're wading through the blood of
Irishmen.

I'm your fellow countryman. Look at me, smell me, hate me
for it, hate me the more because of it – but with me too it's
the heart over the head, the churning in the gut.

I *belong*. My people *belong* and we have been all the way back.
Don't tell me and mine you've got the Holy Word, prior
claim, natural right – and all me and mine are is a two-finger
sign saying No, Against.

And don't tell me, when you've bent and twisted the words
you hide behind so far they don't even make sense to yourself
any more, don't tell me you deserve it because you want it
more than me and mine. Because the first man that said it
was one of my sort, O'Neill of the O'Neill.

(*Swinging round on* **Naylor**.) History again, your favourite
subject. Or maybe just a story but what the hell, so long as
the story's a good one and one well told. The mists of time.
The whys and wherefore. Long-off tales of far ago. Ten
centuries ago – (*Snap of his fingers.*) that long ago, when the
High Kings of Ireland dwelt in marble halls and your
forebears were still squatting in mud huts beside the Thames

waiting for football to be invented so you'd have something
to do with your brains – the land of Ulster is up for grabs.

Fair country. Place of mists. Hard men. Women who are
brightness of brightness and crystal of crystal. Ulster the
Jewel in the Irish Crown. The first man to put a hand on the
North keeps it. Neck and neck around the final bend.
'Faster,' says O'Neill of the O'Neill to his sweating oarsmen,
ribs snapping, eyeballs bursting, you get the picture – (*At*
Naylor.) You wouldn't know this of course Mr Naylor,
you're from a nameless people going nowhere, you've no past
that echoes, no future that haunts you – but the O'Neill takes
his battle-axe and severs his hand at the wrist and throws it
on the beach.

You understand? The Red Hand of Ulster. The Red Hand
on the flag we fly. The Protestant Red Hand that says 'I'm
here and you will never bomb me out'.

What's that? Trust a Paddy to prove his case by going back
a thousand years? What would you know, son, whose past
stops at last week's football results, whose myths are
American imports on the telly and whose nearest thing to
poetry is the bingo caller's patter?

(*Back at* **Roche**.) Here we are and here we stay, in the ditch
with you, clang on the head for clang on the head, until
we've got the boot on your neck again and this time, you
Fenian bastard, you're never getting up.

A quiet moment and then **Roche** *speaks, as if a decision has long
been made.*

Roche   Now you've got that off your chest and all – I'll take
that cup of tea.

A beat as **Nelson** *recovers, controls himself, acknowledges the shift in
relationship.*

Nelson (*to* **Naylor**)   You heard the man. He'll take that cup
of tea.

Naylor   Standing orders sir.

Nelson (*to* **Roche**)   How do you like it?

Roche How about on a silver tray at the Ritz?

Nelson Thick enough to stand your spoon in?

Roche Four sugars and one for luck.

Naylor Beg pardon sir –

Nelson Three sugars for me. Easy on the milk.

Naylor Can I buzz the cell-block duty, sir? Behind you, on the wall?

Nelson The big red titty on the wall? That's when you're in trouble, man. Never the problem, is there, Roche?

Roche Never the problem from where I'm sat, no.

Nelson You'll have that cup of tay, won't you? And the chat?

Roche It'd lay the dust. And if you've something to say, I'm going nowhere the next couple of hours.

Naylor Then it's never the problem. Is it, Naylor?

Naylor (*reluctantly*) Two cuppas sir, yes sir. Milk and sugar.

Roche Well . . . let's be getting on . . .

The lights black off on **Roche** *and* **Naylor** *as an alarm bell rings insistently. When it stops ringing* **Nelson** *and* **Harris** *are alone on stage, under the blow-ups.*

Harris Harris on. In like good old Wally Flatfoot with his belching gut and bike clips. Taken note. Taken note this is not as per. Something still doesn't add up here. Figuring the angles. Wishing it were a straight brutality. Hoping it were but knowing he's missed something. Some Turd Comet From The Planet Mars is hovering around him, too.

He looks at **Nelson**.

Harris Harris on and has to get stuck in because he specialises in anti-terror with them whose bleeding accents strip the paint from doors, those city rats and farmers' sons.

Nelson *sits behind the interview desk, in the same chair we've seen* **Roche** *in until now.*

Harris   He took the cup of tea. The confusing bastard says Yes on top of all that – that wind and spittle.

Simple soldier, ballot and the gun, risen people, never in a million – then he says Yes please, I'll lay the dust with a cuppa. You got him where you'd been pushing him.

And after all that work, that hooking, baiting, playing – you hit him. So I've got a pair of confusing bastards here. A matching set. His and Her Confusing Bastards and there was me looking forward to a nice night in and here I am instead.

Anyone expecting a call? Back home? Check in do you, on the hour, something like that, let the missis know?

We could do that for you. Never easy being a copper's wife anywhere these days. What the missis have to put up with – savage amusement. (*Pointed.*) Why don't you tell me about your missis, Nelson?

Nelson   It'll be in there.

Harris (*checking file*)   English girl. Where did you meet her?

Nelson   Out.

Harris   Not your average copper's missis. Or maybe. I don't know. Is there an average cop? Especially your side of the pond.

I need help. Because every time I think I'm just about to get in behind the Irish eyeballs of one of your sort, you confusing bastards blink.

Nelson   But you keep trying.

Harris   Paid to, aren't I?

Nelson   You keep chasing after, half a mile behind.

Harris   Wally Flatfoot me. I'm no star. I have no track record of turning hard cases a hundred and eighty, getting

is Can it really be you take that as a compliment?
stroll on over me.

on Perhaps we do. A cultural phenomenon.

is But your missis learned the hard way they was the
site to a compliment –

on She'd throw them at me like the dinner plates, like
omestic china, yes.

ays What about the wilderness in here, thumping that
y heavy chest of hers – Is there nothing there but ice
tone? What are you, the Bitter Lakes, the Salt Flats, the
rs of the Moon?

is Well they probably talk like that at Queen's
ersity, don't they? There's a lot of literature about.

what and however, hard for you to take after a wet day
a walking target.

on Hard to take and then some.

ly, taking his measure of **Harris**.) There is something about
rand of bully boy that irritates the hell at the best of
, isn't there?

brand of Brit, our brand of Prod – no, I'm not talking
t irritating the hell out of Roche's mob, that's just hate,
's no harm there – that irritates the hell out of *you*.

g the worst of yourselves in us. Not comfortable to live
are we? The clockwork Orangeman, bobbing behind
ribal banners, our ranting reverends, ya-hooing down
teer, so damn confusingly loyal to you we'd blow up
last one of you if we had to –

is I really don't want to talk about your ranting
ends and your tribal banners, DI Nelson.

Londoner, mate, and I resent what's basically a
rel between two brands of Irishman has done to my
, my life, both as a copper trying to do his job and as an
ary fucking human being.

hat? Chew on that, *Pat*.

fellas to turn in their best pals, their brothers, their very own
grey-haired granny.

That's a very special skill and I have no special talents. Just
an ordinary copper me who'll put in his time and turn his
pension into a country pub with roses round the door.

Nelson Lovely.

Harris It will be. Me and the missis, bless her, starting
over. (*The file again.*) You did very well for yourself. Got a
photo of her, have you? In the wallet? Or is it safer not?

Nelson Safer not. But I can tell you she's a pair of fine big
bruised thumbs of nipples on her and all, just where they
should be too. If you haven't got that down there, too.

Harris I'll take your word.

Queen's University, Belfast. Department of English – what's
this?

Nelson Literature. They can't get enough of it.

Harris Well now here's a novelty. A big tough cop like you
and someone with the education to know better. Her bit of
rough were you?

Nelson Some of them like it rough.

Harris Turned on by the flak jacket, was she, and the
bulge in your trousers that turned out to be, to her great
disappointment, your hand-gun?

Nelson Whatever you say, sir. Fine by me.

Harris I'm looking for an out, Nelson. For us, for our good
name, but also for you.

Nelson I hit him. What else is there to say? Statement – 'I
hit the wee bastard' – End of Statement. I'll sign that. Now
charge me or put me on the next plane out.

Harris Two seats behind you could be Roche, free of all
charges.

You know what spineless bastards they can be upstairs when there's a hint of brutality. Even though they have the forensic they could dump the whole prosecution.

Nelson   Be a pity that.

Harris   It would be.

Nelson   But I can't help you.

Stalled, **Harris** *goes back to the file.*

Harris   Your missis must be a bit of a worry to you. Her and her boyfriend.

Nelson   Now that's a bobby dazzler of a file you have there.

Harris   You're in mucho trouble, pally, and not just matrimonial.

(*Leafing through the file.*) What is this peculiar fascination your missis has with the Irish, Nelson? First you, then the one she left you for. (*As if distracted.*) I don't know if I locked that bloody car door or not – (*Back at* **Nelson**.) Nigger lover is she? Has a thing for the natives? Loves the blarney and the sense of danger?

Nelson   We're charmers – till you get to know us.

Harris   An educated woman like that, falling for a bit of rough like you, then this other nigger. It does happen. It's been remarked on. It's a cultural phenomenon, that's what it is. Educated tart away from home fell for a nigger from the bogs, did she?

Nelson   I thought with you specialising, you'd know better –

Harris   Doesn't it happen? It does happen. The well-bred fanny itching for a bit of black. The English rose who creams herself at the thought of being slapped around by a nigger from the bogs.

Nelson   It's that word nigger.

Harris   *Sir.*

Nelson   Sir.

Harris   It upsets you?

Nelson   That's the point. No. We don't share particular itch with you. Maybe because we hav bunch to be getting on with hating. So nigger do you.

Harris   But you bit.

Nelson   I did? I don't think –

Harris   I think you did. I think you bit.

Nelson   Well – she was my missis.

Stalled again, **Harris** *tries once more.*

Harris   This other nigger, he'd be from Roche' town, am I right? This O'Brien character, who's your missis these days –

Nelson   Statement starts – 'I hit the wee basta Statement ends.

Harris (*ploughing on*)   She fell for you, thinking falling for all the laughing boys under the blue s lethal charmers. Only she finds out too late ther of Irish. The laughing boys and the bully boys a what she has?

Nelson   She'd pulled herself a Proddy.

I'll give you some words for Proddy. Narrow, b ambitious and tough. How about – 'a grim, ste powerful for good and evil? Relentless, revenge suspicious, knowing neither truth nor pity?'

Harris   I'd go along with those.

Nelson   Teddy Roosevelt's words. He also sa Protestant Ulsterman, 'for all his many failing men the best fitted to conquer the wilderness'.

Harris   Lovely. Now was he on your side or

Nelson   Just what the missis asked.

Nelson   Have I bit? Or have you? What do you think, Mr Harris, sir?

Harris (*controlling himself, fighting for the initiative again*)   And off she goes with O'Brien, the other sort of Irishman, the roaring boy out of the lazy South.

He's got his sneakers under the table while you're out getting shot at. You're protecting his civil rights and the bastard's enjoying your conjugal ones. Hard to take, that.

Nelson   I should have known something was up.

Teach Yourself Gaelic on the bookshelf, cheap reproductions of Jack Yeats' muddy daubs around the house, the gee-tar thrown over for the penny whistle and a bad case of the Celtic Twilights.

Not to mention her sudden disinclination to wash her hair or get out of bed, mornings.

Harris   Before you know it, Jumping Jesus there's O'Brien in the sheets between you, sucking on those smashing boobs.

Nelson   But that wasn't the worst of it. Not enough that Laughing Boy from the Bogside is there in the bunk with her, but he starts her on the accordion.

Adultery's one thing but I will not have that instrument around the house. The rest I could handle but a man can only take so much. It's out of the house that afternoon and never set eyes on her or him since.

Harris   Not until you walked in on Roche and there's O'Brien.

Nelson   Spitting image, to the life and more than flesh and blood could take.

Harris   Be handy that, wouldn't it? If that was how it was.

I could build on that. I could make it something personal, something matrimonial. You wouldn't come out smelling of roses but I could get your bollocks off the barbed wire at least.

Nelson   I don't think so.

Harris   I could make it work.

Nelson   And wouldn't you like to get in between us, doing what you do best –

Harris   Yes or no?

Nelson   You have my statement if you want it.

Harris   Somebody's got to get between you, haven't they?

Nelson   You won't be there for ever, Mr Harris. One of these days you'll pack up and go and it'll be us and them, me and him and we'll know what to do.

You think it'll be over when you pull out? It'll be Game One.

Harris   That's what you want, is it? That's what you're aiming for?

Nelson   I'm aiming to get to the end of the week in one piece, week after week. My horizons are sadly limited.

Harris   And this is what we can expect, is it? When you and him are left alone? With nobody to ride shotgun on your interviews? When this is what happens?

Nelson   But you still don't know *what* happened, do you? And you couldn't understand it if you did.

Harris   Try me.

Nelson   We're going to be sold down the Swanee, one of these fine days. Or should I say the Shannon? You'll bolt, like you bolted from every place else, leaving a smash behind.

I'm not so daft as to believe you won't dump us when it suits you, too. And who'll be picking up the pieces, then?

Harris   You?

Nelson   Think this is a war? Think this is news? Wait until the gloves come off. Wait till you scuttle home and Roche's boys come down from the hills with a four-hundred-year chip on the shoulder and find us waiting. We *will* be waiting.

Harris   That's why you did it? Dry run is it? Putting down a marker?

fellas to turn in their best pals, their brothers, their very own grey-haired granny.

That's a very special skill and I have no special talents. Just an ordinary copper me who'll put in his time and turn his pension into a country pub with roses round the door.

Nelson Lovely.

Harris It will be. Me and the missis, bless her, starting over. (*The file again.*) You did very well for yourself. Got a photo of her, have you? In the wallet? Or is it safer not?

Nelson Safer not. But I can tell you she's a pair of fine big bruised thumbs of nipples on her and all, just where they should be too. If you haven't got that down there, too.

Harris I'll take your word.

Queen's University, Belfast. Department of English – what's this?

Nelson Literature. They can't get enough of it.

Harris Well now here's a novelty. A big tough cop like you and someone with the education to know better. Her bit of rough were you?

Nelson Some of them like it rough.

Harris Turned on by the flak jacket, was she, and the bulge in your trousers that turned out to be, to her great disappointment, your hand-gun?

Nelson Whatever you say, sir. Fine by me.

Harris I'm looking for an out, Nelson. For us, for our good name, but also for you.

Nelson I hit him. What else is there to say? Statement – 'I hit the wee bastard' – End of Statement. I'll sign that. Now charge me or put me on the next plane out.

Harris Two seats behind you could be Roche, free of all charges.

You know what spineless bastards they can be upstairs when there's a hint of brutality. Even though they have the forensic they could dump the whole prosecution.

Nelson   Be a pity that.

Harris   It would be.

Nelson   But I can't help you.

Stalled, **Harris** *goes back to the file.*

Harris   Your missis must be a bit of a worry to you. Her and her boyfriend.

Nelson   Now that's a bobby dazzler of a file you have there.

Harris   You're in mucho trouble, pally, and not just matrimonial.

(*Leafing through the file.*) What is this peculiar fascination your missis has with the Irish, Nelson? First you, then the one she left you for. (*As if distracted.*) I don't know if I locked that bloody car door or not – (*Back at* **Nelson**.) Nigger lover is she? Has a thing for the natives? Loves the blarney and the sense of danger?

Nelson   We're charmers – till you get to know us.

Harris   An educated woman like that, falling for a bit of rough like you, then this other nigger. It does happen. It's been remarked on. It's a cultural phenomenon, that's what it is. Educated tart away from home fell for a nigger from the bogs, did she?

Nelson   I thought with you specialising, you'd know better –

Harris   Doesn't it happen? It does happen. The well-bred fanny itching for a bit of black. The English rose who creams herself at the thought of being slapped around by a nigger from the bogs.

Nelson   It's that word nigger.

Harris   *Sir.*

Nelson   Sir.

Nelson (*pulling back, tightening his mouth again*)   Charge me or put me on the next plane back home. I'm supposed to be on leave.

Harris   I particularly don't want to hear about your leave, Nelson –

Nelson   I've odds and ends to tidy up, cards to write, a wreath to be paid for. Compassionate leave. Death of father. Five days back.

(*Watching as* **Harris** *grabs the file again.*) Not in there yet?

Harris (*taking his time, sensing the balance is finally shifting in his favour*)   I lost my old fella two years back.

Nelson   There's a lot of it about.

Harris *waits.*

Nelson   The first leave I've had in . . . since Majorca. After the divorce.

I saw to all the arrangements myself. Went off in a very decent manner. And I know what I'm talking about when I'm talking funerals.

Harris *waits.*

Nelson   You see, you have to be bothered with the hows and whys, the back in the mists of bleeding time.

Harris   Seen much of the old fella, the past couple of years?

Nelson   Saw him over here, as matter of fact. Civil Servant. Northern Ireland Tourist Board. Now there's a bunch of optimists for you. You know the difference? A pessimist thinks things can't get any worse –

Harris   An optimist knows sure as hell they will, yes.

Nelson   He was doing a big Holiday and Leisure show. They'd stuck him in the far corner by the fire doors, well away from everyone else. That old bald guy. Unclean. That old bald guy my dad.

Harris   Never thought I'd miss my old bugger.

Nelson   I'm used to the horrors. I walk through them every day. I'm used to what are more the acts of beasts than men, though that's unkind to beasts. But to come on my old man, no one within a mile of him –

Harris   Miss the old sod? I do, something rotten.

Nelson   That hatchet face? The one before me in the line of grim men that add up to me?

Who knew there was a chance, who said there was a chance but ended up marching along with mad eyes and pinched together bums to the music that says 'We're pissing in the gale of history and while you're at it, here's a fart for commonsense, here's a fart for the inevitable – not to mention the Bishop of Cork.'

Here we come, swinging down the road, defying you to prove us wrong. Here we are and here we stay and na na na na na na na na na na na na na na na na na na and na na na and every time there's half a chance it's on with the bowler and out with the shooter.

Harris   And never an end to it, right? We pull out, the gloves come off for real?

Nelson   Never an end to it. A condition. Like the weather. No end to it.

Harris   He knows this. Roche. He knows what's coming. Right?

Nelson   Oh ay. Don't flatter yourself – you're the warm-up bout. We've seen nothing yet, the real hard cases.

A hesitation from **Harris**.

Harris   Tell me about that cup of tea. Tell me why you had to get him alone?

Nelson   Come on now. There's some things you can only do with the shades pulled down. You have your pride.

Carefully **Harris** *pushes further*.

Harris   Just buried your old man, collared back off leave to do the job you're best at. He says he'll have that cup of tea, and there's the two of you, alone –

Nelson   Nelson on. Doing the old song and dance again. Doing the thing I have a gift for and so, in his bent way, has Roche.

(*Needing him to understand.*) Here's me, do you see, me and Never-the-Problem Roche and I've got in behind his eyeballs and here's that wise man my dad, who pulled on the bowler once again and tried to swagger with the rest of them. That wise and funny man, who ended up another pisser in the wind, he's here too –

And I'm bellowing at Roche, the Orange gorilla – 'Here we are and here we stay in the ditch, in the ditch with you, you Fenian bastard, clang on the head for clang on the head and this time you're never getting up.'

Me. That wise and funny man, I like to think, but don't we all. I'm in the parade with all the rest of them, bellowing out that fart defiance, that strapping fella, me.

Harris (*carefully, again*)   And Roche says? The bit we don't know. After Naylor left?

Nelson   He says – 'Well, let's be getting on.'

Harris (*puzzled*)   'Let's be getting on'?

Nelson   And here we go again, the same old jag.

I turn him and take the next plane out and what's been solved?

Me, in the parade with all the dead men, a little deader every day than I was the day before. Madder. Balder. Pissing in the gale. The rat in my head shut up.

And there's his smirking, knowing face. He knows exactly how I'll jump. He'll go along, in his parade, like me in mine. He'd got me by the throat like I'd got him.

And I hit him.

Harris   Not in anger? It was not in anger?

Nelson   There was anger. Yes indeedy. But not for Roche.

Harris   Not in anger but knowing it would wash the prosecution down the pan?

Nelson   No anger in that moment, for the man Roche.

Harris   But knowing what it would do to the case?

Nelson   You say –

Harris   Hit him where it would show, knowing –

Nelson   You say –

Harris   Turning on your own –

Nelson   He's my own.

As the words hang in the air, **Harris** *turns to* **Naylor**.

Harris   He will not help himself. Nor us. But he's one of ours, let's keep that well in mind. He's one of ours and we have to know our loyalties, don't we?

Naylor   Well, I got mine well straight now sir, just about. Since you said something could be done.

Harris   Medical job.

Naylor   You say?

Harris   Got to be.

Naylor   Tell me. Sir.

Harris   State of him. Pulled back off leave. Should not have been let near.

Naylor   Wobbler? Threw a wobbler, sir?

Harris   Out of his tree. Overwork, most likely.

Naylor   (*considering it, cautious*)   Him off and whistling. What about me, sir? That doesn't help me.

Harris   You buzzed the cell-block wally like the smart kid you are, reporting your concern.

Naylor   Concern sir. Yes sir. What concern would that be then?

Harris   Nelson's mental state –

Naylor (*as if trying it on for size*)   Buzzed the cell-block wally –

Harris   And he didn't show. So you went looking and we'll get you off all charges without a stain on your underpants.

In fact, I shouldn't be surprised if you don't get a recommendation and a choc bar. Which could be very nice, with your board due.

Naylor   Well, stroll on over me.

Mornings I wished I had not got out of bed, days I wished I had not been born. Life, leave it out, I said – and now I'm clear of everything, after all.

Coat sir? Did you have a hat?

After a beat **Harris** *turns to* **Nelson** *again.*

Harris   Straightforward assault, in mitigation your personal circumstances and outstanding record. I'll build the file for you, put in the fix. On condition you resign the service, after decent interval. Fight it and we'll have your pension, really fuck you up.

If it gets to court we'll back you all the way – handwritten testimonial from Jesus Seamus Christ himself, get you off with a warning, outstanding officer all that crap.

On condition.

That you bury this.

(*Controlling his anger.*) We wanted Roche. We had him. He'll walk. He'll go free. Those gutless bastards upstairs will never wear it because if we brutalise him in the cells what's to stop us planting the gear in the first place?

You're resigning. Print that on your Irish eyeballs, pal.

Nelson   Oh, I'll crease the half sheet all right –

Harris   Do that and waltz right out of it.

Nelson   Hardly waltzing.

Harris   You have had your confusing little moment.

Nelson   Indeed I have.

Harris   And not so little, neither. Two years of police work down the drain.

(*Summing it up, under control.*) I got one for you. Don't stop me if you've heard it.

Mrs Brown's having terrible trouble with Little Jimmy and Little Timmy. 'You got to do something, George,' she says, 'I asked them what they wanted for supper just now and they said bleeding fish and chips, of course, you silly old bitch.'

Dad gives them a clip round the ear and puts them on notice – 'Starting tomorrow morning anybody uses a swear word in this house gets the back of my hand, I mean it, think well on.'

Next morning he turns to Jimmy – 'Now Jimmy, what would you like for breakfast?' 'I'll have the fucking cornflakes, you silly old bleeder' says Jimmy.

'Right' says Dad, picks him up by the ears, throws him across the room, kicks him into the street, pulls off his belt and gives him a thrashing. Breathing hard, he comes back into the house –

'Now,' he says to Timmy – 'what would *you* like for breakfast?'

'Well' says Timmy – 'I'd be a cunt to ask for cornflakes, wouldn't I?'

(*Close in on* **Nelson**.)   Don't be a bigger cunt than you are, Nelson. He's not your own. We are.

Nelson   Is that right?

Harris   I gave my fucking career to anti-terror. I lost good mates. I saw things I never wanted.

Nelson   You're a true believer, Mr Harris. Maybe I can't be that any more.

Harris   What's it all been worth, otherwise? What's been the point?

Pulling back, a shaken **Harris** *takes his coat from* **Naylor**.

Naylor   It's the diet I reckon sir. I reckon they don't eat right. Ever known a Paddy eat a proper meal? Salad? Nice bit of fish? All those fry-ups and mugs of sweet tea? Could be some sort of explanation, good as any.

Harris   But then, you don't intend to specialise.

Naylor   Not me sir. I like getting home nights and switching off. I never saw it as my job to bang their fucking heads.

Harris   I'm not sure that I do any more.

Naylor   But the bit of glamour on anti-terror, sir? And the extra allowances? Be fair –

Harris   It'll see me up to the engraved tankard and handshake from the Commissioner. And you're signed up on it, too.

Naylor   Me sir? Babby here? No way.

Harris   Once a year my son, or more, until your engraved tankard and handshake you'll be signed up looking for some poor bleeder's missing arm or head. Maybe a pal of yours, who knows? You're in the ring and no one cares that you couldn't be less dead uninterested in the hows and whys and the back in the mists of bleeding time.

As they head offstage together –

Harris   I shouldn't sit next to beery flatfoots in the canteen. You want a drink, your daddy'll buy you one. And put you right on one or two things, meantime.

(*A last, bitter, uncomprehending look at* **Nelson**.) Paddies?

I can smell them. Animals they are.

Nelson   There was nothing said but 'Let's be getting on'. Sure, what could be said, him to me, me to him. The crime is breathing.

Roche *again.*

Roche   A straight brutality it was, on the jumping bleeding heart of Jesus. My crime is breathing, for the likes of him –

Nelson   Because that would say I led him on and he listened and that could get him killed.

Roche   Your man's not just a thug in size fifteens, you're saying? That one of his sort could break step with all those hatchet heads? He meant to get me off?

Nelson   He can't afford. Come on now, do you want to get him killed?

Colour starts to glow as the entire back wall becomes a montage of the hills and loughs and cliffs and narrow lanes and green glens of Ulster, the object of this passion, cockpit of this hate.

Roche   We've another date, him and me. When the Brits pull out. When the gloves come off.

Nelson   We've another date. Him and me.

Roche   Night or morning, down a lane.

Nelson   Down a lane or in the street.

Roche   You've seen nothing yet.

Nelson   Game One, indeedy.

Roche   Down from the hills, out of the back streets with a chance to finish it. A chance to put it right for once and for all.

Nelson (*echoing the words, with a different tone*)   A chance to finish it. A chance to put it right for once and for all.

Roche   He won't be making jokes then. Good or bad. Not when the gloves are off. When the chin wagging's done and it's him and me.

The colours glow brighter, a tin whistle plays hauntingly, reminder of the beauty at the heart of both men's obsession.

Nelson   Me and him. And half a chance to put it right. And no gags then, good or bad.

Roche   And who'll be laughing then?

That's him. The blue Sierra with the roof rack and the yellow plates. Two hundred yards, by the gate, facing this way. Blue shirt, brown slacks, open neck. Tan jacket.

All Ulster behind him, at peace having come to this place, a moment of stillness –

Nelson   Pat and Mike are ordered to bump off this RUC man, but he doesn't show. 'Dear God' says Pat to Mike, 'he's late. I hope nothing's happened to him.'

Nelson (*a final look at* **Roche**, *all hate gone, all anger spent*) Sure, if you didn't laugh, you'd cry.

He's alone on the stage with **Roche** *as the lights slowly fade, with the music playing, and the waiting* **Nelson** *is the last thing we see . . .*

ROYAL COURT WRITERS

*The Royal Court Writers Series was launched in 1981 to
celebrate 25 years of the English Stage Company and 21
years since the publication of the first Methuen Modern
Play. Published to coincide with each production, the series
fulfils the dual role of programme and playscript.*

The Royal Court Writers Series includes work by

Karim Alrawi
Thomas Babe
Sebastian Barry
Neil Bartlett
Aphra Behn
Howard Brenton
Jim Cartwright
Anton Chekhov
Caryl Churchill
Sarah Daniels
George Farquhar
John Guare
Iain Heggie
Robert Holman
Ron Hutchinson

Terry Johnson
Manfred Karge
Charlotte Keatley
Paul Kember
Hanif Kureishi
Stephen Lowe
David Mamet
Mariane Mayer
G. F. Newman
Wallace Shawn
Sam Shepard
Sue Townsend
Timberlake Wertenbaker
Snoo Wilson

Methuen Modern Plays

include work by

Jean Anouilh
John Arden
Margaretta D'Arcy
Peter Barnes
Brendan Behan
Edward Bond
Bertolt Brecht
Howard Brenton
Simon Burke
Jim Cartwright
Caryl Churchill
Noël Coward
Sarah Daniels
Nick Dear
Shelagh Delaney
David Edgar
Dario Fo
Michael Frayn
Paul Godfrey
John Guare
Peter Handke
Jonathan Harvey
Declan Hughes
Terry Johnson
Barrie Keeffe
Stephen Lowe

Doug Lucie
John McGrath
David Mamet
Patrick Marber
Arthur Miller
Mtwa, Ngema & Simon
Tom Murphy
Peter Nichols
Joseph O'Connor
Joe Orton
Louise Page
Luigi Pirandello
Stephen Poliakoff
Franca Rame
Philip Ridley
David Rudkin
Willy Russell
Jean-Paul Sartre
Sam Shepard
Wole Soyinka
C. P. Taylor
Theatre de Complicite
Theatre Workshop
Sue Townsend
Timberlake Wertenbaker
Victoria Wood

For a Complete Catalogue of Methuen Drama titles
write to:

Methuen Drama
Michelin House
81 Fulham Road
London SW3 6RB